About the Author

Lemuel R. Boulware is a native of Springfield, Ky., and a graduate of the University of Wisconsin, where he taught accounting and commercial law briefly after graduation.

For his services as Operations Vice Chairman of the War Production Board in World War II he was awarded the Presidential Medal of Merit and a citation by the Navy.

In the course of his business career he has been a public accountant, a purchasing agent, a comptroller, and a factory manager, and then successively marketing manager of the Easy Washing Machine Company, vice president and general manager of Carrier Corporation, vice president and general manager of Celotex Corporation, and vice president and general manager of General Electric Company's wholly owned manufacturing subsidiaries.

As vice president in the relations area for the 14 years prior to his retirement from General Electric on January 1, 1961, Mr. Boulware helped GE pioneer new concepts and practices in its relations with employees, unions, stockholders, governments, and community neighbors.

Mr. Boulware is the holder of four honorary degrees: Doctor of Science, Doctor of Humane Letters, and Doctor of Laws (2).

THE TRUTH ABOUT BOULWARISM

trying to do right voluntarily

The Truth About Boulwarism

Trying to Do Right Voluntarily

by Lemuel R. Boulware

The Bureau of National Affairs, Inc. Washington, D.C.

Printed in the United States of America

Library of Congress Catalog Number: 77-91413

To

GEORGE H. PFEIF

with admiration, gratitude, and affection
for his guidance, strength, and credibility,
which so importantly influenced
what is reported here.

CONTENTS

FOREWORD

This account has been prepared in response to requests—which surprisingly persist after eight years of retirement—for more authentic reference material on the employee and community relations work with which I was associated from mid-1947 through 1960.

These requests continue to come from business school and other students—as well as from their teachers and even their parents—who want information for theses and classroom discussions, who find too little available in the course materials or in the school and city libraries, and who judge what they do find to be predominantly the work of opponents of this controversial program rather than those who sponsored and ran it.

This same desire for a better balance of material on the subject is reflected in the speaking invitations I still receive from faculty and other campus groups, in the requests from dictionary people that I define "Boulwarism," in the requests of three universities so far that I bequeath them my personal "papers" or files on the subject, and in continuing questions I get from both relations specialists and the daily press when the term is brought up in negotiations in various industries.

Incidentally, this "Boulwarism" is a term devised by others and continued in use over the years by them. The title and preface of this book represent my first use of the word in print. When asked in the past for my impression of what was meant, I always replied good-humoredly that it seemed to be a term invented and promoted by others largely in an attempt to use a bad-sounding name for that very good thing which was General Electric's program of trying not only to do right voluntarily in the balanced-best-interests of all concerned but also to make sure that all those affected so understood.

What is offered in the ensuing pages is intended solely as a report of what I was trying to do to help General Electric both deserve and achieve the cooperation of its employees and neighbors in their own interests as well as in the equitable interests of the others involved. It makes no pretense at being an adequately organized or professionally written book in the usual sense, but is simply a narrative with some illustrations of the text and drawings used in the program. It presumes to offer no advice to students or others as to what they should do now.

It is a chronicle not of individuals but only of past ideas and efforts. To avoid diverting attention from these ideas and efforts, there was initially no mention of the names either of those who were in disagreement or even of those prized former associates who were so helpful but whom I might thus inadvertently appear to be involving in responsibility for the inevitable imperfections of the recollections here recorded. As I went along, however, it became impossible to resist the mention of my oldest surviving associate, George H. Pfeif, who not only was among those most helpful throughout but also now, at a hale and hearty 85, is beyond all possible controversy while still an embodiment of that earned credibility that we were all trying to merit.

It runs to such length because my correspondence and contacts keep indicating the need for a quite detailed explanation of the background of many of the ideas and efforts that I had taken for granted were long since understood on the campus as well as by the public press.

Its immediate purpose is to meet the existing demand described above. However, I must admit to the hope that it may serve the larger purpose of helping to clarify the events of a period when private business had inexcusably lost its way with the majority of the public and had, thereby, let the misled majority prevent private business from being as useful as it could and should have been to the whole public in both material and nonmaterial ways.

This has been a private personal project undertaken entirely for the reasons given in the first three paragraphs above. I hope it will in some measure recapture past exciting times for any of my old associates who read it. But it has in no sense been initiated, sponsored, censored, financed, or otherwise aided by General

Electric, although the company naturally was asked, and it graciously gave, permission to quote any of the employee and community relations material for which I was responsible in the period covered. Actually, it is in large part an assembly of such material, some condensed and some quoted in full. The rest has been set down to record views accumulated mostly in my 50 years before going to General Electric—that is, when I was in school, in the army, in teaching, in wartime Washington government work, and in service with five other companies.

The whole is offered, for what it may be worth, as a seemingly needed and desired addition to the educational material available about a past program of such continuing current interest. Any royalty has been foregone in order to enable the publisher to offer the book at a lower price, and to bring its availability to the attention of more students of the subject, than would otherwise have been possible.

Lemuel R. Boulware

July 1969

1 THE ASSIGNMENT

Late the last Friday afternoon in May 1947, I was surprised to be handed the job of finding a more rewarding approach to General Electric's employee and community relations problem. I had had no previous professional service in this field.

My business experience had been in accounting, production, marketing, and general management. This had been in accordance with a career plan suggested by a wise and revered professor in the fall of 1915. Upon learning that I vaguely thought I would like to become a general manager in a manufacturing company, he said in substance:

> "It's very simple. You go first through the 'money' area of business—accounting and finance—both because that will give valuable experience there, as well as furnishing a window into the other areas, and because it is the lowest paid. Then, second, you go through the 'things' area—engineering and production—because that is the next most challenging area and the next lowest paid. And then, third, you go through the 'people' area—selling customers, employees, and others—because that's the most challenging and the best paid of the three. Finally, if you have shown reasonable promise in each of these three areas, some company will then—if its distress is great enough—risk trying you out as its general manager."

This incident is mentioned here because of the implication in the professor's words that customers and employees were to be treated the same. This advice had been received but it had not registered. Thirty-two years later, however, it would come vividly to mind in connection with the new job.

I had had a dual assignment during the 29 months since I had come to General Electric. One duty was as marketing consultant. The other was as the parent company officer having staff responsibility for the seven wholly owned manufacturing companies, which had 16,000 employees and were doing business at a $150-million annual rate.

1

In the transcriptions of talks made to management groups at several of the larger parent company plant locations in 1946, this identical paragraph appears as the last of nine reasons given each time as to why General Electric kept these as separate corporations:

> 9. The interest of General Electric in the study of decentralization of responsibility and authority. Little competitors of General Electric kept being successful, despite General Electric's presumed advantages in reputation, engineering, financial strength, and in other directions. General Electric management wondered why and wanted to know why. General Electric was particularly interested in observing how different would be the methods and results of General Electric trained men and of executives acquired outside when these men were enjoying that measure of independence and authority usually given a corporation president and the department heads in a small to reasonable size company.

Each of these seven affiliated companies had a full-fledged president—with these five vice-presidents reporting to him:

Vice-President—Engineering
Vice-President—Manufacturing
Vice-President—Marketing
Vice-President—Finance
Vice-President—Employee & Community Relations

This last-named position reflected, back there, a very significant departure from prior practice in and out of General Electric. It had naturally been quite a mental and emotional wrench for many of the managers, professional specialists and others—who had been going conscientiously about their work as they saw it—suddenly to have to face the now obvious fact that the employee and community relations function not only had been too long neglected at all levels but also had become, if it had not always been, equal in importance to engineering, manufacturing, marketing, and finance.

It was one thing to establish the position. It was quite another to fill it. There were no ready-made professionals with broad enough training and experience to meet the greatly increased scope of the new requirements. But able and eager candidates had shown up and were expanding their knowledge and skill as fast as could be reasonably expected. And all the affiliated plants had run full and without incident during the parent company's seven-week strike in 1946.

It was only this too brief and slight experience with the affiliates that gave me any inkling of what the new assignment was really going to involve.

What I was being told that day in 1947 was that General Electric simply had to correct the ridiculous situation where—despite the best of intentions and the best practices known—the company was distrusted and disapproved of by employees and neighbors in some very important matters, as recent events had so clearly demonstrated. I was told to find out what was wrong and come up with a program that would utilize in employee and community relations those principles and practices that had been found successful in dealing with people in other areas of the business. The program should avoid doing in employee and community relations what had not worked or would not work successfully in the other areas. The plain inference was that we must be acting unnaturally for businessmen in the troubled area, as contrasted with our acting naturally, as successful businessmen do, in the other areas.

I was urged to forego consulting with other people* in the field, as they were practically all showing the same strange lack of success as General Electric. In fact, I was told my lack of previous experience in the new field could be an asset if it meant a really fresh scrutiny of what was going on.

With this as my charge, I faced a busy weekend before stepping into the new job on Monday morning. There, I was sure, I was going to find reason many times to be thankful that I had long ago taken the "expendability vow."†

---

* I confess to having disregarded this advice at once, and the very significant results of that interview will be related later.

† A term meaning a commitment to fulfill one's responsibilities in great causes regardless of the possible consequences to oneself.

2 THE MISSION OF BUSINESS

To act naturally in the employee and community relations area—in the way we or other successful businessmen did or should in the other areas—it would be necessary for every General Electric manager and specialist involved to keep clearly in mind—and help all others concerned keep clearly before them—the unique purpose, nature, and mechanics of ours as a private business.

A privately owned business is a voluntary association of people doing things for each other. They voluntarily choose to associate because they can thus do more for each other than if each were working alone. They are able to do more for each other because the manifold contributions of investors and managers—ideas, designs, materials, facilities, coordination, subdivision of operations, opportunity for specialization, and risk-taking ability and willingness—so "lengthen the arms" of the individual that his output is many times what it would be if he were working independently and alone with the aid only of the ideas, materials, tools, facilities, skills, and other resources that he could bring to his work.

A private business is not just buildings, or machinery, or inventory, or money. Business is primarily people . . . . dealing only with each other . . . . with each willing to provide equal value in return for what he wants. Business thus concerns itself with things only through people . . . . and then only as the result of people indicating they need or want those particular things.

One of the top marvels of all the world's history is the way we interdependent citizens have come together in business voluntarily, have so largely done for each other what each wants done in return for what he provides, and have in the process maintained our education and morals at a level that permits almost everybody to go around doing practically as he pleases without intruding unduly on the free-choice and other rights, dignity, usefulness, economic progress, and spiritual well-being of his fellow citizens.

I think the real mission of General Electric or any other private business—as well as a requirement for its survival—has been and is to please people by helping them get all they have come, on the basis of enlightened understanding, reasonably to expect from the business in both material and nonmaterial ways.

But in 1947 the majority of the public was obviously dissatisfied in some very important respects with the performance of private business in general and of General Electric in particular. Despite all we had accomplished for the good of all concerned—and all we had tried to accomplish beyond that—we decided that, in our case, some considerable part of the dissatisfaction simply had to be well founded, while the rest would prove unfounded when the facts were known. Both kinds of dissatisfaction, however, were primarily the fault of us managers.

It took only the briefest of research to bring to light three important areas of neglect and failure:

First, we had failed to explain convincingly to enough people how our practices and results benefitted the many and not just some few, as was claimed by the opponents of private business.

Second, we had not begun to exhaust the possibilities both of gearing our intentions, practices, manners, and results as intimately as we could and should to the other fellow's viewpoint and of making him not only hear but see and feel that we were doing so.

Third, our most damaging failure had been neglecting to help misled people to adjust their expectations to what was reasonably possible and feasible at the moment. This failure by ourselves—and others—had let people acquire, retain, and act on misconceptions about business which were the same kind of uncorrected misconceptions they had about government. People in the main—and even most college graduates—here and around the world had built up a preposterously false expectation not only about what government could by some magic "give" the individual citizen with little or no expense to him but also about what business could deliver on that same something-for-nothing basis. This resulted in too many people assuming that there was "more in the wood" than there currently was or could be, that somebody was getting enormously more than his rightful share, that management could deliver vastly more benefits if it were willing to do so.

To go realistically at any correction of the above—and to seek to win the trust and cooperation so necessary to General Electric's usefulness to all concerned—it was going to be necessary to face and correct the deeper problem presented by the belief of a majority of employees and neighbors and more distant voters in these three economic, political, and moral misconceptions—which incidentally, the majority did not realize were basic socialist teachings common to all the various brands of socialism:

1. That the owners and managers of private business are brutes and crooks.
2. That a privately owned business is simply a privileged racket for exploiting the deserving but helpless many to get profits for the undeserving but powerful few.
3. That gang force—rather than individual persuasion or individual worth on a willing exchange basis—is the way for the individual to get what he wants.

There were demagogues in politics, as well as charlatans in other areas, who knew better but made a business of capitalizing on this misinformation and the resulting emotions. But they were few in number compared with the great public majority of honest and otherwise intelligent people and their thought-leaders who sincerely believed—from both wishful thinking and an absence of corrective teaching—that these socialist teachings about private business had some foundation in truth and even that they themselves had seen or sensed some concrete evidence to that effect.

To remedy this situation and get the cooperation needed toward the good ends of the business, it was going to be necessary to analyze more carefully than ever before just what it was specifically that people were demanding of business. Then we would have to fill that demand to the extent that we could under the circumstances and fill it in *their* way. And then we would have to become competent and warmly persuasive in helping all concerned to understand not only when the limit of feasibility had been temporarily reached but also that it would do them harm rather than good in trying to get more by resorting to force.

3 WHAT PEOPLE WANTED

The people who did things for each other in private business then, as now, did so in five contributor-claimant roles: investor, customer, employee, supplier, and neighboring or more distant citizen.

The whole of what they were demanding of business—including demands that were realistic and those that were unrealistic—seemed to be made up essentially of these three:

1. The basic material satisfactions
2. The extra human satisfactions
3. The assurance that the balanced-best-interests were being served.

To get at the specific dissatisfactions of individuals—and the degree of validity or unrealism in each complaint—we had to examine more closely their reactions in their various interdependent relationships in the business—that is, in the one or more of the five roles in which each was acting as a contributor and corresponding claimant.

The new program in the beginning was to deal only with the employee and the citizen. But, for purposes of perspective, all five are described here along with what each seemed to want. Incidentally, they are not given in any order of importance; all were interdependent and equally essential.

1. Investors

Our shareowners were the citizens who had saved rather than spent some money. In response to an incentive—which may or may not have been as good as it seemed at the time—they had risked their savings in the investment which had made the very existence of the business possible in the first place. They were the contributor-claimants who made service to customers possible, made jobs possible, made sales and jobs for other supplying businesses possible, and made General Electric's location in and services to given locations and the nation possible.

It was very obvious that the owners of private business were the many and were not any few, as the critics of business were so often trying to make out. I do not have the exact figures for 1947, but 10 years later the direct investors in private business looked like this:

8,630,000 individual citizens who owned stock in the country's leading corporations listed on the stock exchanges

1,400,000 who owned stock in smaller or other corporations not listed on exchanges

3,500,000 unincorporated businesses owned by more than that number of individuals

5,000,000 farms, which were businesses, of course, and which were owned by more than that number of citizens.

Then, in addition to these more than 18 million direct owners, there were these further millions of savers who were indirect investors because their funds were being risked in business securities whose worth depended on the health of the economic and political climate for business:

15,000,000 participants in private pension funds
109,000,000 insurance policy holders
91,000,000 savings account depositors
42,000,000 other personal bank depositors

Of course, that half of our country's population who were homeowners had had the same incentive to forego current spending and to save and invest—and had the same interest in the protection of their private property—as did the direct and the indirect investors in private business.

Naturally there were, in the above figures, many cases where people had invested their money in more than one form of ownership and were therefore counted more than once. But evidence is still clear that the overwhelming majority of adults in this country must have been in 1947, as they were 10 years later, either direct or indirect investors in private business. Farmers, teachers, clergymen, professional people, widows, and business proprietors, as well as the others who made up the 1947 work force of 70,000,000—including hourly workers—had some or most of their savings at risk in private business and "working for them" there.

There were relatively few rich people among these owners—and they were becoming relatively fewer all the time—in comparison with the rapidly growing number of owners who were in more modest circumstances.

Yet it quickly became obvious that owners were the most misunderstood of all citizens. Then, as now, there was a tendency to think of them as "bad" people way off somewhere else, whereas any fresh look would quickly show they were the same good folks found all about—folks next door who were not only investors but also workers, consumers, and as good citizens as the rest.

No doubt there were some bad people among them. But it would have been quite surprising if investors' personal intentions, conduct, and usefulness as a group were not up to or even a little above average in view of the good judgment and self-discipline evidenced in their personal saving and investment programs. For instance, two thirds to three fourths of the congregations in most churches must have been made up of families in which the breadwinner was a direct or indirect investor in business.

At the time of the above investment figures, General Electric had 400,000 individual shareowners of record, in addition to the many thousands whose holdings were in brokers' names or in investment trusts. Other trust funds held our stock for the benefit of colleges, churches, and other institutions. About 65 percent of our nearly 250,000 employees were already shareowners or in the process of making the installment payments to become shareowners. Naturally, many of our customers, suppliers, distributors, dealers—and their employees—along with our community neighbors, were shareowners.

Contrary to what had been the too-well-promoted idea that investors are not people at all but some strange, flint-hearted, bloodless beings, our later research clearly showed that our shareowners were natural and normal folks in the best and most human sense of the word. In return for the use and risk of their savings—and for their further contributions through buying our products, speaking well of us, and helping protect our usefulness to all—they typically wanted, in essence, exactly the same things people wanted in the other four roles:

1. *The basic material rewards* both through the receipt of worthwhile dividends and through the protection and enhancement of the value of the savings they had risked on the facilities and plans of the business.

General Electric profit had typically run at five to six cents per dollar of sales, with about four cents going to the shareowners and the balance being used for expansion of the business or to cover inadequate depreciation allowed under the tax laws. This four cents was in sharp contrast to the 15 to 25 cents which too many people in and out of the company were found still to believe the owners were taking out in profit from our company as well as from business in general.

2. *The extra human satisfactions* to be gained from full information, opportunity for significant participation and recognition in matters of the common interest, and a gratifying two-way association in an enterprise whose economic and social objectives and results they were proud to approve and support. They wanted to be fully useful. They did not want to be thought bad people—because they felt they were good people who were doing good not just for themselves but for the many.

3. *The assurance that the balanced-best-interests of all were being served* .... specifically that the good dividends, the attractive growth in the value of their risked savings, and any outside reputation of the business for accomplishments in human betterment had all been the result of competence and diligence applied equally to the interests of all concerned to the extent humanly possible, and had in no instance come from any such thing as "robbing Peter to pay Paul."

2. Customers

Customers were the people who were giving or withholding work .... who were giving or not giving us our daily jobs to do.

While our owners had made our jobs potentially possible, only customers could actually supply and maintain our jobs.

Our customers were free to buy those of our products and services which we were able to offer at values they found attractive and in circumstances they approved. In return for their willingness to buy, they as claimants were demanding in essence:

1. *The basic material rewards* in the desired performance and competitive price of the product or service.

2. *The extra human satisfactions* to be gained not only from the product—because of its form, color, taste, aroma, convenience, distinction, and other emotional or esthetic attributes—but also from our manners in dealing and associating. Incidentally, there were market researchers estimating that we U.S. citizens on the average might be working as little as an hour a day to meet the actual needs of survival, and the other seven hours to satisfy our desire for extra human or emotional satisfactions beyond actual need.

3. *The assurance that the balanced-best-interests of all were being served,* and that the attractive material and human values supplied them as customers were not achieved at the expense of equally fair and attractive arrangements with other customers or with employees, suppliers, distributors, and affected citizens in the proximate or larger community. The "brother's keeper" obligation was both surprisingly and gratifyingly found to be still very much alive, and even the fellow who pushed for and thought he got a "special deal" was quite likely, on sober second thought, both to doubt that it was as special as the deal someone else had received and to want to make legal or market trouble for the vendor.

In our free market and opulent society, the customer had many alternatives to buying from General Electric or from any member of any particular industry. The bulk of his buying could usually be put off for quite some time, and most buyers had seemed long since to have learned that "you can't make a good deal when you are in a hurry." Yet—and maybe for these very reasons—more that was good about dealing with people had been learned and successfully applied in customer relations than in any of the other four. This will be examined at greater length in the later reporting of the new program itself.

3. Other Businessmen

General Electric had arrangements with suppliers, distributors, dealers, and other vendors of materials, components, and services simply because these had proved they could provide the items in question more efficiently than the company could make them using its own employees and facilities. The competitive margins were usually so thin that our business, like any other, could not long survive if it should attempt to do in its own facilities the kind and amount of work that other businesses could do better. Just one important reason for this was that these more economical and efficient outside sources were also available to, and being used by, our competitors, who would most surely keep on using them to our competitive disadvantage. General Electric had at the time 500 major competitors and thousands of smaller ones competing for the sales we needed to keep us going.

In addition to outside help in the distribution area, we were buying from over 40,000 suppliers of materials, components, and services, which alone accounted for from 43 to 47 percent of our annual sales dollar, depending on the product mix. We were thus in somewhat the position of being responsible for their volume of business and jobs, and of guaranteeing the quality of those parts of our products which had been supplied by them. Many of these suppliers—as well as the distribution people—were located in communities where we had substantial operations.

Both the suppliers · and the distribution folks seemed to want—in return for what they did for us—the same from us as the contributor-claimants did in the other four roles:

1. *The basic material rewards* in a profitable opportunity and in the steadiest feasible use of their employees, facilities, and specialized skills.

2. *The extra human satisfactions* to be gained from full information, respect for dignity and human values, significant two-way participation and resulting deserved recognition, and an association that would yield mutual rewards both in increased business competency and in heightened kindredness of spirit.

3. *The assurance that the balanced-best-interests of all were being served* .... specifically, that both the attractive profit opportunity and the rewarding personal association were the product of able and faithful creativity in serving the interests of all

on a two-way, something-for-something basis, and were not the result of "robbing Peter to pay Paul."

4. Employees

Our employees were doing the work needed to be done within the Company's own facilities. And that work had to continue being done better than we could get it done outside—and done better than competitors could get it done inside or outside their facilities—or the jobs of our employees would disappear.

Certainly, therefore, wise and conscientious employees would—when fully aware of the facts—want to contribute their full skill, care, and effort to the common end of pleasing people not only with the attractiveness of the values we could offer but also with the way we had conducted the business in achieving those values.

In succeeding chapters there will be more detailed explanation both of what we found to be our problems in employee relations and of what our research and experience led us to do. At this point it seems necessary only to report that our early inquiry brought to light the obvious fact that our managerial, professional specialist, white collar, and blue collar employees wanted— probably by now to no reader's surprise—just what other people had been found to want in their contributor-claimant roles. In return for their skill, care, and effort, they wanted:

1. *The basic material rewards* in the right pay, benefits, physical working conditions, and other financial or material aspects of their jobs. (Employee compensation characteristically took about 40 cents of the sales dollar.)

2. *The extra human satisfactions* in such things as important work, respect for dignity, full information as to what was going on and what lay ahead, participation and recognition, and a gratifying two-way man-to-man association with their supervisors and fellow employees in a common effort of real significance.

3. *The assurance that the balanced-best-interests were being served* .... that their good jobs and good pay and other attractions and rewards were the result of diligent efficiency and not of any short-changing of customers, suppliers, distributors, owners, or citizens.

It took no research to know that here was an enormous problem. We already had ample evidence that the majority of our employees did not think they were getting anything like these three kinds of satisfaction on a something-for-something basis in return for what they thought they were contributing.

5. Citizens

General Electric had contributor-claimants as neighboring or more distant citizens—even though most of them were at the same time found to be customers, many of them to be employees and owners, and quite a few to have family connections with local suppliers and distribution people. We had five to 50 times as many neighboring citizens in our plant cities as we had employees there.

These people as citizens—over and beyond their other roles— were having an increasingly damaging effect on the ability of General Electric to be fully useful . . . . on our ability to do the very things people wanted of us. The lately developed "double standard" of police protection and law enforcement, along with what was taught in the schools, preached from too many pulpits, printed in local and national media, and said on the air—most of it with the best of intentions—was militating against that cooperation by employees and others which would enable us to make the sales that would bring into the communities the increased funds desired for distribution there. Yet, while overestimating their contributions and ignoring the harm done through the deteriorating business climate, people as citizens still wanted these characteristic things in return:

1. *The basic material rewards* in such things as the money brought into town for payrolls and local purchases, the taxes paid, the money and manpower made available for local charitable and civic projects, and the opportunities offered to distributors and dealers.

2. *The extra human satisfactions* to be gained from our keeping human considerations high, from the cleanliness and attractiveness of our buildings and grounds, from the lack of smoke, odors, and noise, from the manners of all responsible employees from managers to truck drivers to telephone operators, and from the feeling that all who really represented the company had the interests of the community at heart.

3. *The assurance that the balanced-best-interests of all were being served* .... that the money brought into town and the other benefits dispensed there had been ethically earned and had not become available through sharp practices or through running roughshod over anybody.

The Score

If people had been formally surveyed in each of their five contributor-claimant roles in 1947, the score would surely have been found, as it was later, to look like this for General Electric—as it also would have for almost any other leading industrial company:

For what they believed to be the value of their contributions,
was General Electric supplying a reasonably satisfactory return
as to:

	No. 1 Basic Material Rewards?	No. 2 Extra Human Satisfactions?	No. 3 Assurance of serving the balanced-best-interests?
Customers thought	Yes	Yes	*No*
Owners thought	Yes	*No*	*No*
Other businessmen thought	Yes	*No*	*No*
Employees thought	Yes	*No*	*No*
The above and others as citizens	Yes	*No*	*No*

Even the 'yes' votes in column No. 1 above would have been hesitant and qualified.

Our customer was buying our products in preference to others. He obviously believed them to be the best values available and worth the money. Otherwise he would have selected alternatives or would have delayed or foregone his purchases. But in the main he unquestionably believed we could offer still better values if we wanted or had to, and he too often suspected that the good values we did offer had been, in greater or lesser degree, made possible by losses or indignities we had inflicted upon others.

Our owners liked the dividends and the prospects for growth in them as well as in the value of the shares. Otherwise they would have sold. But, in a typical year, sales of shares—either to meet a need for money or to switch to another investment—were totalling only about 6 percent of the company's outstanding stock. And there were many trades of the same shares during the year. Obviously more than 94 percent were being confidently held for the long pull. Yet a lot of our investors—and not just because half were women—were asking why we did not pay out a higher percentage of our profit in dividends. The vast majority of them had never seen any of us in management, and, whether for this reason or not, they were nervous about the charges of dishonesty and inhumanity that had been lodged in some quarters against our management as well as others. And too many of them had even been developing a guilt complex about receiving profits claimed to be unearned, excessive, antisocial, and the product of a privileged private business system which licensed the undeserving few to exploit the helpless many. These investors would have liked to feel differently, but, until they had different and convincing information, they could not.

Other businessmen obviously liked the profit opportunities we were supplying by dealing with them at prices that were lower than our own costs would have been using our employees and facilities, yet were high enough to permit them to pay all their expenses and still make a profit. They also liked the way we took on the sales, risk, and responsibility of big jobs which we then broke up into little jobs most of which the thousands of suppliers could do. If they had not liked to do business with us, they would have made themselves unavailable. But we were very big and they were usually much smaller; and—while we were trading with them on the basis of the going market prices at which our competitors could obviously buy and sell—it was very easy for any one of them to feel we could do better in his particular case without much if any adverse effect on our total result. Besides, the otherwise sensible and sophisticated businessman at any level was likely to join unthinkingly with the enemies of the private business system when they aimed their brute, crook, and exploiter attacks at any business larger or more successful than his own. He too rarely sensed that these charges were aimed also at him, were eating into his vitals, and were generally just as false in the case of the larger business as in his own case.

Our employees obviously liked our pay and the other material aspects of our jobs to the extent that they thought them the best available. General Electric had doubled its employment in recent years while other jobs were freely and amply available. But employees thought we could do much better if we wanted or had to. They had been misled into believing that they should resist rather than cooperate . . . . that they could better themselves by being less useful. They had been seriously affected by the constant brute, crook, exploiter charges against private business in general, and we found that about the most we could hope for at the moment was that they regard us as "the best of a bad lot." Most of the balance of this volume will concern this problem, so no more need be said here.

All the foregoing four groups of contributor-claimants together with the rest of our near and more distant fellow countrymen obviously—as citizens—liked the money we brought into the country and into the individual communities. But they thought the business could be run for the greater benefit of the public as a whole even in these material ways as well as in the other nonmaterial ways. A good portion of what follows will have to do with this problem.

The "yes" by customers in column No. 2 will get detailed treatment later. The reasons for the "no" answers in the rest of column No. 2 and in column No. 3—and what we thought could be done about them—will be substantially the same as what is later outlined in connection with employee and community relations.

4 HOW GENERAL ELECTRIC HAD BEEN TRYING

With this combination of some old and some newly appreciated requirements in mind—and in the face of this rather discouraging score as to the related satisfactions and dissatisfactions—let's look at what and how General Electric had been trying in employee and community relations.

Our primary objective, here as elsewhere, had been progress. To pioneer had been our traditional determination. This had applied not only to trying to provide the best values in the best products and services. It had applied also to trying to make and keep jobs good in every proper material and human respect. Likewise, it had applied not only to our bringing important money into the communities but also to our determined efforts to be generally useful as a good corporate citizen there.

For instance, at the time of this 1947 decision that a new and broader program was needed, we looked back not only on having had the highest wage scales that were feasible and proper by all the product and labor market standards, but also to our having voluntarily pioneered our employees suggestion systems in 1906, safety and health programs in 1907, pensions in 1912, savings plans in 1917, insurance in 1920, relief and loan plans in the 1930s, ambitious experiments in work and pay guarantees—including the guaranteed annual wage—in the 1930s, and profit-sharing plans in the 1930s and 1940s.

Not only had we provided good and remarkably steady jobs, but the number of them had doubled in just a single decade. This doubling of jobs, as already noted, was accomplished in a continuing "sellers market" for employee services. Anyone dissatisfied with his job could get another one almost anywhere. Yet we not only kept our old employees but more than doubled the number of jobs. A typically held view was: "General Electric ranks high among corporations in its treatment of workers."*

What was apparently not realized by the employee and community beneficiaries in 1947 was that our pay and benefits had increasingly made our jobs so attractive that many of the communities were already having difficulty both in persuading other employers to expand there and in persuading new ones to move in beside us. For instance, a later (July 24, 1954) Berkshire (Mass.) *Evening Eagle* editorial reported that General Electric was "the employer of nearly 75% of Pittsfield's wage earners" and that "trying to lure new business here . . . . won't be easy."

Starting from scratch 70 years before, we had persevered in pleasing people with our products and services until we were bringing into our communities an overall amount of business activity which had been estimated to be the major support of 40,000 retail establishments; to maintain 1,200 schools with 21,600 teachers; to supply opportunities for 28,800 professional men outside General Electric; to supply dividends to over 1,000,000 people besides our employees and their families; to support the selling and servicing of 540,000 automobiles a year; to mean $240-million of revenue for railroad traffic in and out of the communities; to create a taxable valuation of $3-billion; to give markets for $420-million of farm products and to create an annual expenditure of $1.8-billion in trade in our communities.

What this contribution meant to newspapers, churches, and endless individual enterprises can be well imagined.

Over and beyond all this, our strenuous efforts to wed science with human needs and desires had resulted in our taking still more drudgery out of the work in factories and homes—including the homes and places of work of our employees and our neighbors—as well as helping otherwise to raise the level of living by the additional products and services we were enabling more and more people to buy.

As already noted, our activity also benefited thousands of other businesses, particularly the smaller ones, through our taking on large assignments and then breaking them up into smaller

---

* "How Collective Bargaining Works," Twentieth Century Fund (1942).

assignments which could be carried out by smaller or more specialized suppliers not in position to get the orders directly.

Furthermore, the technology we continued to pioneer, while spreading across our own growing industry and across the whole of industry here and abroad for the good of all, had been ever on call as an important factor in our country's military security. Indeed, General Electric had played a spectacular role in the World War II production miracle which had earned for the American business-man the eternal gratitude of the free world.

And our presidents and board chairmen—along with countless others of the managerial, professional, and other members of the General Electric family—had always been freely available and had served with distinction in our country's emergencies in peace and war over a long period here and abroad.

Yet, as we have seen, all this had not been understood. It had not resulted in employees' and neighbors' approving our accomplishments or even having a sufficiently favorable attitude toward our efforts obviously in their behalf. It had not resulted in job satisfaction or community satisfaction. In fact, the harder we had tried and the more successful we had been in bringing in the benefits, the more misunderstanding and disapproval we seemed to experience.

Evidently the misunderstanding had been most pronounced among us managers—and at all levels. We just did not know the nature and dimensions of the difficulty we had continuously tried to remove by incorrect or inadequate or paternalistic means. The recognition of this is what had brought General Electric to the decision to institute a more penetrating search for the facts and then to pursue as comprehensive a program of action as might be indicated.

5 THE SEARCH

Both the initial look around our business to see where we had been most successful in dealing with people—and the sudden recollection of my professor's unheeded advice of 32 years before—suggested that the principles and practices in marketing should be examined for possible use in employee and community relations. Despite our still only qualified success with the customer as to requirements nos. 1 and 2—and our failure so far as to no. 3—we had nevertheless been about twice as successful with the customer as we had with any of the other contributor-claimants. And a good part of this success had obviously been due to our organized attention over the preceding 20 years to the extra human satisfactions in this area.

Prior to 1926 the practice too generally across business had been for an inventor or some engineers to design a product, for the production people to build it, and for it then to be turned over to the salesmen to sell. There was some informed reporting back by salesmen as to the customer likes and dislikes that had lost them orders. But it was a hit-or-miss procedure, and too often the customer had had a choice only between competing products which the makers had largely turned out *their* way. A history of The Marketing Executives Society says:

> For the most observant, there had occurred back there in 1926 the final confirmation of the revolution from the old "me" kind of *selling* to the new "you" kind of *marketing* with emphasis especially on pre-sales preparation extending to the product as well as to the other elements in sales planning. The final evidence of this change had been in Ford being forced at last to abandon the famous old Model "T"—which had been made the way *he* wanted it—and to come out with the Model "A" which was made the way the *customers* wanted it.

The budding new *marketing* profession—as the successor to what had heretofore been *sales management*—was developing out of the "me" to "you" revolution . . . . and consisting of

Market Research
Product Planning
Sales Planning
Sales Organization and Related Distribution Structure
Sales Training
Dynamic Pricing
Advertising and Sales Promotion
Servicing to Satisfy Old Customers and Make New Ones

The big change was in expanding the scope of Market Research and in employing the quite new Product Planning. Market Research had, in general, been confined to the *statistics* of where and how big the market was, who was getting what portion of it, and what were the immediate sales prospects ahead. Now the more alert and forehanded marketers were adding the all important *qualitative* function of finding out what customers liked and disliked about one's own and his competitors' products and services, what would be *better* liked, and what price would pull at the time the appropriately revised offering could be put on the market. A most essential fact to be ascertained here was *what the prospective customer wanted, and would pay for, beyond the purely functional and in the extra emotional satisfactions to be derived from form, color, aroma, comfort, convenience, fashion and status.*

It is perhaps hard to realize in 1962* the extent of the consternation which was then caused by the earlier practitioners who were emboldened by this new kind of information to come home to the new Product Planning sessions and lay down the law to engineering, production, financial and even general management as to just what the basic function, the extra features, the appearance and the price of the new models had to be a month or a year hence, or else they would not be salable.

General Electric had, of course, been developing and practicing this new kind of product marketing for 20 years. It was aimed at persuading the prospect not only to buy but also to enjoy all the assurances and continuing satisfactions rightly to be derived from the transaction and the subsequent ownership. Fortunately, we *wanted* to do this. But even if we hadn't, it would have been a sheer necessity for survival in competition.

What we had first to examine was whether we could just as sincerely and effectively employ these same tried and proved

---

* The year the history was written.

product marketing methods and considerations in genuinely pleasing people with jobs as we had now for so long in pleasing people to so high a degree with products.

Could we use these same principles and methods in job marketing, that is, in periodically designing, soundly pricing, accurately presenting, and actually delivering and servicing "new model" jobs which not only would deserve to achieve—but also would succeed in achieving—the maximum job satisfaction available within what we could help be recognized as the feasible, and only really possible, return for employee contributions on a something-for-something basis in the balanced best interest of all?

Could we pass on to our employees—our "job customers"—the benefits of what we had learned in many years of pleasing product customers through the application of humility, ingenuity, and diligence to market research, to product planning, to sales organization and training, to personal man-to-man information transfer, to the use of mass communication to supplement the man-to-man process, and, finally, to servicing the inevitable customer complaints? We decided to try.

Could we use these same tried and proved product marketing principles and practices in trying to deserve and get the corrected understanding, the warm approval, and the mutually beneficial cooperation of our communities? Here also we decided to try.

6 JOB MARKETING

Our objective here was employee cooperation. We wanted first to deserve to have—and then to have—our employees want to abandon their misled resistance, which was estimated by our top management to be keeping output at least 20 percent below what it would be—with no one going home tired—if only the employees understood that it was in their own material and nonmaterial interests to cooperate. Incidentally, this 20 percent estimate was shown many times to be way, way low. Managers, employees, and community neighbors—once they knew the truth about this waste and its consequences to all of them—would surely cooperate to eradicate it.

The best approach, we believed, was to start with a job-marketing program that was as close as we could possibly come to an exact copy of the principles and practices we had long used with comparatively good success in meeting our customers' requirements for (1) the basic material rewards and (2) the extra human satisfactions. However, it was going to be necessary to do these things more thoroughly—or to take additional steps—not only in order to be more completely successful than product-marketing had been in (1) and (2) but also to become deservedly successful in supplying (3), the balanced-best-interests assurances. This was going to take a lot of doing, because our product competitors were nowhere near so economically and politically powerful—or so unsound or untruthful—as were our ideological competitors, who were causing the cooperation slippage through the false credibility they were getting for the brute, crook, and exploiter charge against us as well as against private business in general.

So, with high appreciation of the diligence that was going to be required, we took the first step: job research. We went out to ask our employees what they wanted in their jobs and how they felt their present jobs fell short of their desires. We tried to diagnose what they consciously or subconsciously liked and disliked about their jobs; what they understood, misunderstood, or just didn't know or ignored about their jobs. We inquired into what they did and did not understand about the economic, social, and political influences which surrounded their jobs with opportunities, obligations, and limitations.

We looked for the motives and beliefs which determined whether they came to work promptly, regularly, and in an agreeable mood; the things that determined whether they gave their full interest, skill, care, and effort while working, and the events and impressions that determined whether they went home reasonably satisfied with their accomplishments and associations at the end of the day.

7 THE NINE-POINT JOB—OLD AND NEW

This search for the facts—via the same depth-interview method used in product marketing—resulted in the clear indication that General Electric employees wanted their job package filled out to contain nine distinct ingredients, to each of which real attention would be continuously paid. They wanted

1. *COMPENSATION,* which includes:
   a. Pay that is right—all things considered—for the skill, care, and full day's effort as measured by reasonable modern standards, and
   b. Extra financial benefits such as pensions, awards for ideas, free life insurance, scholarships, and paid vacations.

2. *WORKING CONDITIONS* which are as good as they can be made at the moment, which are regularly improved, which are being constantly studied for further improvement, and about which all suggestions as to additional improvements are always welcome.

3. *SUPERVISION* which is:
   a. Competent technically to aid the employee to get the most out of the machine or other facilities with reasonable physical effort, and
   b. Competent as a leader to make the employee understand promptly, clearly, and easily the reasons behind the direction or advice given so that he can do his job intelligently and voluntarily, and
   c. Competent as a counsellor or as a guide to good counsel where the employee seeks aid in personal matters.

4. *JOB SECURITY* to the greatest degree possible through the teamwork of employees, management, stockholders, and loyal customers.

5. *RESPECT* for basic human dignity which is protected along with the rest of the employee's stake as a free, upstanding, good American citizen.

6. *PROMOTION* as fast as opportunities arise or can be created and on a strictly fair basis in view of the skill, care, and effort of the individual employee, with the employee's own ability and ambition being aided to every extent possible by training on the job.

(Specimen illustration from employee publication)

7. *INFORMATION* on management's objectives, plans, problems, successes, and failures, and current expectations for the section, the department, and the company as a whole.

8. *BELIEF* in the individual job's importance, significance, and challenge, and in the employee's contributions to the great good accomplished by the final G.E. product.

9. *SATISFACTION* that comes from going home to the family after a day's work with the feeling that something important has been accomplished, that the accomplishment has gained the attention and earned the respect and gratitude of one's fellow employees at all levels, and that the job is a good one to return to the next and following days.

To our embarrassment there was obviously nothing here but what we had intended to provide all along and had blindly taken for granted we were supplying. So we advised all employees on October 15, 1947, that we were going to redouble our efforts . . . . that these announced nine-point job ingredients "are not new at General Electric . . . . *but today they are being pushed more aggressively than ever.*" We were going not only to continue supplying such a package but henceforth, with the aid of constant two-way communication, to try to keep it more intimately in step with the expressed wishes and reactions of employees. Our employees, in turn, had indicated they were perfectly willing to pay the proper price in interest, skill, care, and effort—provided only that they could be confident they knew what that proper price was and knew that the deal was fair all around.

8 BALANCED-BEST-INTERESTS

To deliver satisfactions to employees to the limit feasible under this nine-point job program—and to have them recognize when and why that limit of feasibility had been reached—were dual problems not only of equal importance to both managers and the managed but also of equal difficulty to managers and the managed.

But there was no escape. Fortunately, again, General Electric wanted to give the basic and the extra satisfactions, and wanted to operate in the balanced-best-interests of all. On top of that—even if it had not wanted to—it would have had to operate that way. Despite the company being run by human beings who were not omniscient, both General Electric's desired objective and its survival necessity were one and the same: to try to operate as closely as humanly possible to what was in the balanced-best-interests of all the contributors to and corresponding claimants on our output of goods and services, and to try equally hard to make them all recognize that fact.

For these contributor-claimants were, as noted, not only our employees but also—and just as important—our customers, owners, suppliers, and fellow citizens. Each must be dealt with realistically and equitably. Each must do his part and get his proper return. Each must know when he was being fairly treated.

If any one of them was not—or rightly or wrongly *thought* he was not—being properly treated in either the financial or the nonfinancial area, he would leave or otherwise fail to cooperate in doing his part, and not only he but all the other contributor-claimants would suffer. If there were any voluntary or forced attempt to favor any one at the unfair expense of one or more of the others, the attempt was bound to backfire shortly with damage to the interests of the one intended to be favored as well as to the rest of the contributor-claimants.

Thus the material results of employee and other contributions had to go on the market at the prevailing competitive market prices, and had to be rewarded financially with fair shares of what the free customer regarded as the material and emotional money value of what we did for him. This is not to revive the old argument about whether "labor is a commodity"; it is simply to state the obvious: that the material results of a worker had to be sold in the competitive market at the market price a free customer would pay.

In short, General Electric's policy—of trying its level best at all times, to do right voluntarily in the balanced-best-interests of all—was no pious posing for cheap publicity but was a constant one-jump-ahead-of-the-sheriff necessity in order first to survive and then, hopefully, to grow in that usefulness to all which was the clear opportunity if all the interested parties cooperated toward such usefulness.

9 MARKETING THE IMPROVED NINE-POINT JOB

This nine-point job was to be an intimate relationship between two people—the employee and his immediate employer. The then 190,000 General Electric employees, from top to bottom, were broken at each level into groups of 5 to 50, each under some one of the 15,000 supervisors. We wanted each such group's supervisor not only to be its leader in the usual sense but also to be the retail salesman and deliverer of the nine-point job package and, to the greatest degree possible, to be the lone individual to whom the group looked as its "Mr. General Electric"—or, better still, as nearly as humanly possible its "Mr. Everything" as to the completeness and reliability of the information he offered and as to his untiring efforts to be helpful in job-connected matters.

We wanted him to establish and maintain a separate man-to-man relationship with each of the employees in his group. The constant two-way communication in such an intimate relationship should result in the supervisor and the employee each having in his possession—and usually ahead of need—the various kinds of information that were essential to good decisions by both and equally essential to the enjoyment by both of good employee-manager relations.

No matter what product, facility, organizational, or even management-philosophy interpretation might be hanging fire, there was to be no confusion, uncertainty, or hesitation about its being the job of each individual manager at each level to secure the understanding and cooperation of his 5 to 50 employees. This responsibility had been once and for all delegated to him for as long as he had those 5 to 50 employees. Anything which needed correction, and which he could not get done within his delegated authority, simply had to be pursued up through his immediate boss—and by his immediate boss on up from there, if necessary.

The Supervisor's Guide

To help him in actually providing this improved "new model" job and getting the proper return from his employees, we did the research for and then issued a "Supervisor's Guide to General Electric Job Information." This 120-page manual was supplied to 12,000 foremen and 3,000 other members of the managerial family. It dealt with the new nine-point job, with what was expected in return, with the principles and problems of the leadership or selling involved, and with the overcoming of objections—curing the "don't likes"—which the supervisor was likely to encounter.

Great emphasis was placed on leadership or salesmanship or the improved managerial skill or whatever else would mean that combination of competent teaching and crisp direction, on the one hand, with the fairness and patience and genuine warm friendly interest, on the other—or those qualities and acts, whatever they were, which would make the individual nine-point job customer want to do what the supervisor asked because he had come to recognize it as being in his own interests as well those of all the others involved.

In illustrating this in our training meetings at the turbine plant, for instance, we tried to picture to the foremen how thoughtfully, painstakingly, patiently, and pleasantly our sales engineer went about giving a turbine customer the information and guidance that would cause the latter of his own free will to want to do what we recommended as to the selection of the equipment and the signing of the order. We emphasized the good that the sales engineer does—for the customer, for the turbine-plant employees, and others—by so ably representing the strength and spirit of General Electric with the competence of his information, the confidence he had instilled in the customer, and the genuine, warm, continuing interest he took in the customer's surely getting not only the proper long-time material return on the transaction but also the just as necessary emotional rewards.

The last 95 pages of the Guide were devoted to overcoming employee objections to giving full skill, care, and effort. The survey had collected hundreds of "don't likes" and other reasons for not cooperating fully. These were expressed in a great variety of ways but seemed in each case to mean one or more of only 10 things. Detailed suggestions as to what the supervisor could do and say were given in connection with each objection, but they are too lengthy to include here. The following 10 objections—with an example or so under each—should give enough of a perspective:

1. *Don't like my pay—*
   a. Wrong rate on a plant basis
   b. Wrong compared to other pay in the community
   c. Wrong because pay should be nationally based

2. *Don't like to give my full skill, care, and effort*
   a. Want to spread the work
   b. Fellow employees don't want me to
   c. Job is monotonous and fatiguing

3. *Don't have to give my full skill, care, and effort*
   a. Am protected whether do good job or not
   b. Can get another job just as good

4. *Don't understand how to give work expected*
   a. Don't have skill—need more training

5. *Can't give full skill, care, and effort to my work*
   a. Sick
   b. Broke
   c. Worried over family or other troubles

6. *Don't dare do what's expected*
   a. Fellow workers bring pressure against
   b. Outsiders bring pressure against

7. *Don't think it would do me any good*
   a. All that I get is wrung out of management on a mass basis, and what I do individually has nothing to do with my progress.

8. *Don't like the working conditions*
   a. Place not sufficiently clean, light, airy, healthful, cheerful, or of proper temperature and humidity
   b. Parking facilities bad

9. *Don't like the management here or nationally*
   a. Just orders me around instead of explaining why—could make as good a decision as management if I knew the facts

    b. Manager I see is just a tool setter and work assigner, and has to go to somebody else for any information or decision I want

10. *Don't like the company*
    a. Big business is greedy and unprincipled—has gotten big at cost of workers, consumers, and small businesses
    b. Has monopoly on item after item and can charge any price it pleases while seeking to pay starvation wages
    c. Big businesses abuse their power over little businesses, competitors, and rest of the public

The actions and answers—suggested for each of the above samples and the other variations under 10 headings—had been developed to help the individual supervisors at each level remove any warranted as well as unwarranted doubts and suspicions, give reliable information about company policies, practices, problems and results, illuminate and explain the economic considerations which had to determine what was feasible on a something-for-something basis for all concerned, and, where necessary, to contribute any further sophistication required.

The top officers studied the Guide together. Then each of the vice-presidents held a conference with the small group reporting directly to him, and so on down the line to and including the 12,000 foremen.

How Our Business System Operates

Then DuPont graciously allowed us to use its excellent flannel-board course in economic study and discussion entitled "How Our Business System Operates." This course was conducted in three 1½-hour sessions on company time for small enough groups to provide full participation until all the 190,000 employees from top management to the last nonsupervisory worker had had the advantages of this study in their own interests as well as of the others who benefited from the company's activities. How valuable we judged this to be was indicated by our spending far more than $2,000,000 on the paid time of our own employees in the internal sessions. We were so impressed with the corrective helpfulness of the course to all concerned that we went beyond and offered our own discussion leaders to conduct it in any schools, churches, clubs, or other businesses in our plant cities. One of our discussion leaders was busy for more than a year with such initial requests and with many enthusiastic repeat requests to train the recipients' own discussion leaders.

How You Really Earn Your Living

Subsequently we distributed thousands of copies of Professor Lewis H. Haney's book, "How You Really Earn Your Living," to supervisors and other sponsors of study and discussion groups in our plants and offices and in our plant communities. These excerpts from the author's introduction indicate its scope and purpose:

> This is an American primer of economics. It is written for Americans with the idea of stating the elementary principles of economic life as it has grown and developed in America. It therefore is based upon conditions such as have helped in the upbuilding of this country.

> Americans all have the same real ends: we all want well-being and a reasonable amount of happiness. We all want to be fair and to do the right thing in our relations with one another. We want equal opportunity. We want our rights and are willing to do our duties.

> Accordingly, each point made in the following pages is to be read in the knowledge of the author's sincere desire to find and point out the best way to attain the ends we all desire.

Below is a composite of remarks from typical reports of experiments by amateurs at running the Haney discussion groups:

> "We got six couples to join up for 16 Monday nights. Told them they could drop out if they didn't like it after two or three sessions. Only one did stop.

> "We met at our house after dinner, with one baby sitter for all the kids who were parked upstairs.

> "I opened the session by saying that I was not an economist but a draftsman, as they all knew; that I didn't necessarily endorse or even pretend to understand all that was in the Haney catechism I had in my hand; that I thought the book raised the right questions that fitted in with our immediate everyday problems and general curiosity about things that puzzled us at work, at the store, and in politics; that I didn't think we could settle the problems raised or even always agree on the answers we would *like* to find true; but that, as we went along, I was sure we would gain a helpful insight into most of the questions and learn the answers to many.

"I then read off the question: 'How are wars financed and paid for?' and asked those present to suggest some answers, which got everyone into the discussion. I then said, 'Here's what the fellow that wrote the book has to say,' and read off the half page of comment, after which those present commented in agreement or disagreement or in any other way they liked.

"As this was a fairly noncontroversial matter, I passed on to another question, 'Where does the government get money?,' and asked the wives for the answer. Having exhausted their initial ideas, I read Dr. Haney's page of explanation, and the participants individually expressed agreement or disagreement or discussed additional ideas.

"Without attempting to force any unanimous conclusion, I then passed on to seeing if we could find out 'Why government borrowing at the banks is dangerous.'

"This process went on throughout the 16 sessions with little change. The first two chapters were tough going, but it got easier and more interesting after that. Current events were frequently brought up in connection with a particular subject or question at hand, and many brought in newspaper clippings on the subjects we were discussing. Disagreements would be 5 to 5, or 8 to 2, or 1 to 9—but no matter, as we passed on to the next question, with no attempt to force agreement, we found it to be true time after time that subsequent passages would clear up our indecision or differences of the moment.

"*The most interested participants were the wives.* They asked more questions than the men, and they were obviously surprised that their husbands knew the answers to so few of the questions they had associated with their husbands' work or with 'a man's world.' This brought an amusing but significant development—that is, one husband after another came around during the week to borrow the catechism for study, so at the coming session he would not 'look dumber than the other husbands'—a subject that had apparently been under discussion at home.

"Everyone feels greatly benefited by the series of discussions. Learning economics is interesting fun, and anyone can do it by this method. I am going to start another group, and I'm trying to get another couple of the original participants to do likewise."

Then, as time went on, we were recommending to all our managers, and to many other concerned thought-leaders in and out of plants and offices, that they read, study, and discuss further helpful books like these:

"Understanding Profits," by Claude Robinson (Van Nostrand)

"The New Argument on Economics," by Schoeck and Wiggins (Van Nostrand)

EDUCATION . . . OR DISASTER?

HERE — AND ALL OVER THE WORLD — we are in a race between education and disaster.

It's a race we can't win with our *feet*. But it's a race we *can* win by using our *heads*.

We *can* win it if we all apply ourselves to an intensive study of the important facts of life — while there is still time.

We, as individuals, are constantly in a race between education and personal disaster.

As we progress in learning how to make and run more and better machines — thereby steadily raising our standard of living — we have got also to get the additional knowledge, the extra skills that will help us solve the economic and social problems brought on by these very machines — including those resulting from a constantly greater degree of individual specialization.

Just as nations and businesses must, so must we — as individual citizens — seek constantly to master the economic and moral facts of life, learning how we may voluntarily do our part for others so that they will want to do their part for us.

(Excerpts from article in employee publication)

"Economics of the Free Society," by William Roepke (Regnery)

"Prosperity through Freedom," by Lawrence Fertig (Regnery)

"Economics in one Lesson," by Henry Hazlett (Harper —also in paperback)

"What You Should Know About Inflation," by Hazlett (Van Nostrand)

"Failure of the New Economics," by Henry Hazlett (Van Nostrand)

"The Fateful Turn," by Clarence E. Carson (Foundation for Economic Education)

In addition, we recommended to all managers and other concerned thought-leaders that they read the *Wall Street Journal* editorial page every day, Henry Hazlett's and Lawrence Fertig's columns every week, David Lawrence's and William Buckley's columns and editorials, as issued, the *National Review* every two weeks, and the *Freeman Magazine* every month.

"The Road Ahead"

The little book "The Road Ahead" was distributed to all managers as an unpleasant and unpalatable beginning lesson in sophistication as to just how far some trusted representatives and other thought-leaders in high and surprising places were thought to be going in the direction opposite to their professed aims as understood and believed by their followers and supporters.

The Employee Relations News

Then, to try to keep the supervisor alerted to and up to date on the immediate controversial questions which were currently job-connected and already affecting, or likely soon to affect, employee cooperation—and to try to help the supervisor have a ready means for minimizing the bad effects of any misinformation and, if possible, replacing resistance with a new and enlightened cooperation—we started issuing the *Employee Relations News Letter—(For Circulation Among General Electric Management)*. Its four pages were written late every Friday afternoon, then printed and shipped by about midnight to be in the hands of all 15,000 managers on Monday morning.

Only controversial issues of acute current interest from a material or emotional standpoint, or both, were treated. We were trying to arm the supervisor at whatever level to discuss voluntarily, openly, and confidently those matters of real consequence which had been too largely avoided. As it had elsewhere in the midst of any controversy, prompt and accurate information as to the real facts or as to the most considered conclusions available proved to supply power . . . . the power to help the supervisor and his employees to avoid the wrong course and take the right one . . . . power to overcome the otherwise damaging power of antibusiness forces seeking to cut down the usefulness of business while claiming to increase it. There could be no better evidence of the letter's effectiveness than the very public anguish of the knowing and unknowing charlatans who saw it causing their party line to lose its punch.

We had so many requests from columnists, teachers, clergymen, politicians, and other businessmen—including demands from many of those detractors who felt they were the principal ones being affected adversely—that circulation quickly mounted to several times the original 15,000.

Works News

Obviously, most of our job salesmen were starting the broad and intensive study and practice of salesmanship late in their careers. Also, they were going to be part-time salesmen at best, because they were going to continue performing their customary duties, which were still demanding even though familiar.

Besides, it had long ago been found in product marketing that even the full-time salesman who had taken up selling as a profession early in life usually had to have the help of mass communication paving the way for him in order not only to be able to make the sale but to make it economically. That part of any sale which can be accomplished by prior advertising and sales promotion is usually done more economically than would be the case if the salesman were to do that part as well as the residual part that must be done personally.

So we decided our part-time job salesman was inevitably going to need even more prior mass selling and other supplementary support than our full-time product salesman—both to make the sale at all and to make it at a cost that was feasible.

Fortunately, one ready-made means was at hand. All the medium- and large-size plants had employee newspapers, usually spoken of as "Works News." They typically consisted of eight pages in tabloid size. They were distributed to all employees in the plants and offices late each Friday afternoon. Over the years they had proved sufficiently interesting, credible, and helpful to cause practically all employees to take them home and, with their families, to read them over the weekend.

To test the ability of the Works News to help pave the way for our job salesmen, we ran illustrated full-page articles confirming to our employees and their families in detail the prior economic and policy information which would help the supervisor make the sales outlined in the Guide. Here, again, only controversial issues of acute current interest and impact on employee cooperation were treated. Great care was taken to avoid being contentious; instead, the corrective facts in both the material and the emotional areas involved were supplied calmly and pleasantly.

Formal surveys following each of these test pages at the various locations proved from the outset that most employees had read them and found them interesting if not always wholly understandable, did not resent but welcomed our giving them our views directly on the subjects treated, believed we meant what we said whether or not they quite agreed with us yet, and thought we ought to continue them for one or another of two reasons. One of these reasons was the obvious one that the information might be helpful. The other—to our surprise, although perhaps it should have been just as obvious—was that our very willingness to discuss the subjects in the messages showed we had nothing to hide. Without our saying so in the messages, the employees obviously had recognized that we were now openly and forthrightly discussing things about which we had been under attack, whereas our previous silence in these matters had been judged a confession that we knew we were "getting away with something" along the lines charged.

Incidentally, the content of any one of these pages would take a good hour for an expertly trained supervisor to get across to one of his employees in two-way discussion while interrupting the work—at an obvious cost of more than $5.00 even at the rates prevailing in 1947. The page which the employee took home, studied, and discussed with his family couldn't have cost five cents.

So we began the practice of sending a mat for one of these pages to each paper each week. Where the plants and offices were too small to warrant a Works News, we sent enough reprints of the page for each employee. The nature and timeliness of these pages may be judged from these sample headlines:

General Electric Keeps Trying to Make Jobs Better

How Big Are General Electric Profits—Are They Too Big?

Who Told You These Fairy Tales—Do You Still Believe Any of Them?

Should Pay Be Equal Everywhere?

Should Wages Go Up—and Down—With Profits?

Let's See How We All Made Out!

Who is Telling the Truth—and Who Isn't?

What Did General Electric Earn—and Who Benefitted?

Why Are You Paying High Prices? Who's Responsible? What's the Cure?

Whose Promises Were Kept—and Whose Charges Were Wrong?

What is Communism? What is Capitalism? What is the difference to You?

What's your extra pay? What are the hidden "Extras" in your GE pay? How much extra can be added to your regular earnings?

How can we all live better?

Why these messages?

GE reports a *Profit*—and *Progress* for all

We withdraw a statement (we had made a mistake in a quotation, and hastened to correct it voluntarily)

A report on Pay—and Prices—and Job Security

How did we all make out in 1948?

Where the money goes

Jobs depend on Faith

What about Job Security?

What is a speed-up? And what is just an honest day's work?

"I don't want to be agitated!"

Let's learn from Britain
Who wants Profits—who gets them?
Does your job have a future?
High Wages—Low Prices? We can have them!
A Time for Calm Judgment
The "Anxious Bench"
What do we seek? And how much of that is in our own hands?
Two cars in every garage?
Is opportunity dead?
The Bunk
What would you do?
Profit—enemy or friend?
Education—or Disaster?
We will keep trying to do right—about your pensions,
     insurance and pay
GE—The initials of a friend
More Sales—More Jobs—More Pay—More Earnings—More
     Taxes—AND MORE GOOD DONE, TOO!
Doing right voluntarily
Two kinds of work—and pay
The Balanced Best Interests of All
Steady Jobs through Steady Friends

In addition to these pages in the Works News, we used posters, folders, handbills, letters to the home, films, meetings, special campaigns and most of the other accepted means available for disseminating information when particular questions or opportunities arose to make such a course seem mutually helpful to employees and the other contributor-claimants.

Making the Job Economically Good

What we were trying to do in the above dissemination, as well as in the supervisory training, was to insure that both managers and employees would understand "what was in the wood" as fair and feasible at any given moment, and what could be done by whom to increase what was in the wood and thus increase what was fair and feasible for the one by increasing what was so for all the participants.

The foregoing page messages were but "homeopathic" efforts which needed endless repeating through various illustrative ap-

STEADY JOBS
Through
STEADY FRIENDS

GENERAL ELECTRIC jobs have tripled since 1940. We want them all to be steady jobs.

The nature of our equipment and skills makes us unusually subject to widely varying demands from government and business in national emergencies as well as in between.

Yet ceaseless effort and good luck have kept our jobs remarkably steady through the thick and thin of war and peace.

There is a lot *you* can do. You can help yourself have steady work by doing all you can to keep customers buying G-E products. You — or anyone else — can make your job shaky by undermining customer or public confidence in General Electric. So:

- Help our salesmen by providing them with reliable, flawless products that will keep customers buying G-E products.

- Favor G-E products in your own home, and encourage others to do the same.

- Help cut costs and increase sales by reducing waste and spoilage, and by chipping in with good ideas.

- Tell the story of G.E. as a good producer of quality products, good employer, good buyer of local goods and services, good local taxpayer and good contributor and worker in worthwhile community projects.

- Realize the vital personal importance of not letting little differences be magnified into seeming importance, or into the kind of wasteful practices that hinder the intelligent planning and cooperation we must have to attract the sales we need for jobs.

(Excerpts from article in employee publication)

proaches before both managers and employees would be sufficiently unshakable in their understanding of the answers to such
questions in the bread-winning area as the following:

1. *Where does the money in the business come from and where
   does it go; that is, who gets what for what?*

   This was the most important basic subject for communication
   with employees and neighbors. The usual published annual
   statements served the financial community and the larger
   shareowners fairly well. But there was great need for highly
   simplified quarterly and annual statements—and related press
   releases—to serve our ideological purposes with employees,
   neighbors, and voters, along with editors, educators, clergymen, politicians, and even the great majority of shareowners.

   The profit dollars needed to be shown in vivid comparison
   with the dollars paid to employees, suppliers, and government.
   The cents per dollar of sales needed also to be shown for each
   dollar item. In addition, in a year of rising volume and profit,
   it was fatal to fail to remove a lot of misunderstanding by
   showing the comparison between the extra pay which
   shareowners were earning and the extra pay which employees,
   suppliers, and government were getting; and the bigger was
   any employer's sales and profits, the more urgent it was for
   him to show how much more others were getting than the
   owners were. The two accompanying samples indicate how
   simply this could be done.

2. *Where did our jobs come from . . . . what made them steady or
   survive at all . . . . what made them go away?*

   All concerned needed to learn and then be constantly
   reminded that a job depended on two contributor-claimants—
   the investor and the customer—working in a one/two sequence
   whereby the one made the job possible in the first place and
   the other made the job a daily reality.

   The potentiality of a job was supplied by the investor who
   rightly or wrongly judged that there was a better-than-even
   change to make a profit by risking his savings on the buildings,
   equipment, research, inventory, customer credit, management
   competence, employee training, and other such things which
   had to be provided ahead of time in case a customer should
   want to buy something.

Suggestion for routine simplified report:

Who Got What?
Did you get your share?

	Total Dollars in Millions	Cents per Dollar of Sales
During the past year your company received for its products and services	$2,500	100¢
These dollars were used as follows:		
For TAXES—direct federal, state and local	175	7¢
For MATERIALS, POWER, DEPRECIATION INTEREST, etc.	1,175	47¢
For EMPLOYEES	1,000	40¢
For SHAREOWNERS $110 for dividends $40 reinvested	150	6¢
	$2,500	100¢

Suggestion for simplified report in year of rising profits:

More Dollars Came In This Past Year
Let's look where they went

	Last Year in millions	Year before in millions	Extra last year over year before
Your Company received	$2,500	$2,250	$250
Those dollars were used as follows:			
For TAXES	175	155	20
For MATERIALS, POWER, DEPRECIATION, INTEREST, etc.	1,175	1,060	115
For EMPLOYEES	1,000	900	100
For SHAREOWNERS	150	135	15
	$2,500	$2,250	$250

The actuality of a job was provided only by the customer who was able to buy and who decided to buy for logical or emotional reasons of his own. The usual reason was that he needed or wanted the kind of thing offered, liked the particular one better than any other available, and thought not only that the product was worth the price but also that he could not get a better value anywhere else.

If two or more competing products should be thought to represent about the same value, the determining factor was likely to be the manners of the seller. This was a very real consideration—and had been so for a long time, as witness the pleasant legend of the old French shopkeeper who, in trying to impress this point on his young grandson, said, "Be sure to wrap up a bit of your heart in the package and see your customer to the door."

If the customer thought the product, price, and manners were so nearly alike among competitors as to make no real difference, then the determining factor in his decision often was whether he liked or disliked what he knew or heard about a maker in areas beyond his "metal cutting and paper shuffling." A Works News page entitled "Jobs Depend on Faith" was one of the messages that dealt with the stake all of us jobholders had in our company's reputation.

Jobs went away in the reverse order—that is, in the two/one sequence of the customer first and then the investor. The customer would stop giving the jobholder his daily work to do—usually because the plant no longer could offer a competitive value—and then the investor would go broke or withdraw his support because there was no profit possibility, and the plant would stand idle and empty and worthless because it could not be made profitable.

3. *How is profit earned?*

It is earned (or not) by taking judicious risk and making efficient use of the investors' savings in pleasing people within a price at which successful competitors can sell and at which less efficient competitors are always going broke.

Such profit is the driving force toward the greatly desired growth of jobs in number, in attractiveness and in steadiness.

Doing MORE...
for _LESS!_

**Here's how each group fared during the first nine months
of this year as compared with the same period last year:**

GROUP		1950	1951	DIFFERENCE
CUSTOMERS paid us for goods and services		$1,354˙	$1,694	25.1% MORE
FEDERAL, state, and local tax collectors took		114	220	93.0% MORE
SUPPLIERS of goods and services took		627	755	20.4% MORE
EMPLOYEES' compensation took		500	633	26.6% _MORE_
SHAREOWNERS had left		113	86	23.9% _LESS_

THUS, in the first nine months of 1951, General Electric did more than ever before in an equal period for our customers, our federal, state and local tax collectors, our suppliers of goods and services, and our employees—_everybody,_ in fact, except our _shareowners_ who risk their savings in contributing so largely to our current productivity and our future progress and security.

˙All figures in millions

GENERAL ⊛ ELECTRIC

(Specimen illustration from employee publication)

More Sales — More Jobs — More Pay — More Earnings — More Taxes — and MORE GOOD DONE, TOO!

(Specimen illustration from employee publication)

It is the principal force directly and indirectly producing the taxes so eagerly desired by politicians. In short, such profits are not exorbitant, are not a cost but a benefit, are not "stolen" from the customer or employee or supplier or the so-called "common man" but are even the poor man's best friend.

4. *Who pays the costs of business?*
   All business costs—including wages, benefits, purchases, services, taxes, and even charities—must be paid in the end almost entirely by customers and not by owners. Otherwise the values, jobs, and progress—which all concerned want—would quickly disappear.

   When these costs are forced up arbitrarily by a misled electorate's government and its political allies, prices paid by consumers have to go up or there will soon be nothing for the consumers to buy. Yet sales cannot be made at those higher dollar prices—and the drop in sales will make jobs disappear—unless the government rushes at once to cheapen the value of money. And, of course, such inflation eventually loses its ability to stimulate, and there comes to light then the inevitable value-killing and job-killing effect of the improper use of force to interfere with the free market and to put above-market prices on the ingredients which go into consumer prices.

5. *Who pays taxes?* (This was a most fruitful area of economic study, discussion, and mass communication, since it lent itself to easy demonstration of who paid the expenses of business and of how something-for-nothing was not available through government or elsewhere).

   Everybody paid taxes. No few could or did pay the enormous taxes amounting to more than the income of everybody west of the Mississippi.

   The top 10 percent of the citizens were paying only 24 percent of these taxes. The other 76 percent was being paid by the remaining 90 percent of the public, and thus being paid by that vast majority of voters who not only did not realize they were paying such enormous taxes but had even been misled by their trusted teachers and representatives into

(Specimen headlines from articles in employee publications)

WHAT DID
GENERAL ELECTRIC
EARN ?

. . . and who benefited?

Corporate Profits Help Increase
Flow of Income to All Classes

(Specimen headlines from articles in employee publications)

fondly and pitiably believing they were getting back from government far more than they were sending to government.

The citizen, in his role as consumer, footed the bill for all that government spent, and did so—in addition to his direct and visible taxes—either through immediately poorer values, or slowed progress toward future better values, or both. For the cost of government was physically collected from the consumer in three ways:

—in direct, visible taxes, as such, as in the case of income, sales, property, etc.

—in indirect taxes through having those taxes theoretically "imposed on business," such as income, franchise, property, excise, sales, etc., necessarily passed on to him in the consumer prices he paid.

—in indirect taxes through having the brutal tax of inflation collected from him in the higher prices business had to charge to survive, a consequence of government's reducing the value of money in an effort to hide or delay voter realization not only of who was paying for the always-failing something-for-nothing schemes but also of how bad a bargain this continued to prove.

One third of the price of a new or used automobile was tax; only the other two thirds was for the car itself. Three fourths of the price of many liquors, including the cheap ones poor people bought, was tax. There were 151 identifiable taxes hidden in the price of a loaf of bread. Half the price of gasoline was tax.

The further down the income, savings, or even relief scale a citizen was—that is, the poorer he was—the greater was the relative impact on him of the taxes levied on business and of the tax of inflation arising from government cheapening of our money.

When an employee felt his pay was out of line with consumer prices, he had to be shown that this was not due to exorbitant profits but largely to the unproductive costs business had had to collect back in its prices.

THE BUNK

JUST LAST WEEK it was reported that "the biggest single worry now plaguing administration economists" is the increasing refusal of people to risk new savings in helping expand industry and improve its products and services.

It was even hinted that some top union economists also are worried about this and seriously considering coming out soon for *cutting* instead of raising corporate taxes.

But now plans are afoot from many similar sources to lift some excise taxes off individual citizens, and then to add that amount to the taxes which corporations are already paying.

Will lifting these taxes off consumers and putting them on corporations really mean less taxes for you and other individual citizens?

No! That's the bunk!

(Excerpts from article in employee publication)

6. *What caused unemployment?*

Unemployment—or a so-called "surplus of labor"—came from the lower sales of labor resulting from the price of labor having been forced above what the free market could and would pay.

Unemployment also came from the sacrificing of the jobs of the few in order to save the jobs of the many—as, for instance, where an employer's sales and prices were stuck at a practically constant level for four years, while he was being forced to raise pay rates artificially by 5 percent a year. He just had to find ways to "automate" or otherwise kill off 20 percent of the jobs over those four years in order to operate within the prices he could get and to have any jobs at all for the remaining 80 percent of his employees.

Unemployment was, in reality, less a surplus of labor than a shortage of employers which had resulted from the elimination or serious impairment of those incentives and assurances of fairness which individuals had to have if they were going to save up money by denying themselves some current consumption or pleasure and then risk the resulting savings on value-creating and job-providing projects offering what seemed to be a reasonable likelihood of profit.

7. *Would price and other controls cure inflation?*

They could not cure or arrest inflation and would only suffocate or choke the job-providing system to death. The only way to prevent inflation from coming out the consumer-price end was for an informed and alert electorate to force government to stop the unsound practices which put inflation in the cost end of the system in the first place. Our immediate job as to inflation had long since been not just stopping further inflation but going on to repair or undo the past damage by cooperating in the creation of newly attractive values for foreign and domestic buyers—values that would be good enough to cure the foreign-market, unemployment, and even so-called automation problems.

The foregoing were only seven random samples of the kinds of material issues as to which corrective treatment was needed for all concerned. A wealth of further help was afforded by the references already cited and by new publications constantly being made available.

But just as much needed by managers and other employees was a deep understanding that the nonmaterial benefits from the intelligent operation of our free-choice economy and of our profit-and-loss private business system were even more important and rewarding. And the very process of achieving these nonmaterial benefits, so rewarding in themselves, would contribute to the attainment of more of the material benefits desired by all concerned.

Especially needed in this connection was widespread understanding—and continuous reminders—not only of the morals and ideals required in a free society but also of the resulting edification of the human spirit. Thus, in our publications to managers and employees—as well as in our training and personal contacts—we kept trying to place proper emphasis on

- —the nature of our freedom and its nonmaterial as well as material value.
- —the rewards of accepting and carrying out individual responsibility.
- —the exalted spiritual returns from applying zeal to excel in an atmosphere where worth rather than force is the incentive; and where such worth is determined by that individual free choice which is the conspicuous difference between our system and that of the collectivist opponents of private business.

We needed to learn and teach that our freedom was not given to us and was not safe—that it was not won from George III for all time—but could and would be enjoyed only by citizens who would do their individual part in investing in its very worthwhile price every day.

We also—and most especially—needed not only to learn and teach the moral ideal of freedom but also to live by the moral requirement which must be met. For, if we were to be free to go around doing largely as we pleased at and away from work—and were not, in the process, to interfere with the rights and just deserts of others—the vast majority of us not only had to come to

FOR EVERY DOLLAR RECEIVED
during January, February, March...

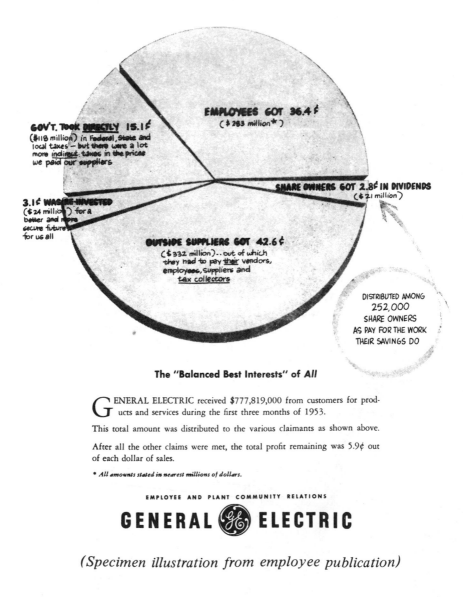

EMPLOYEES GOT 36.4¢
($283 million*)

GOV'T. TOOK DIRECTLY 15.1¢
($118 million) in Federal, State and
local taxes – but there were a lot
more indirect taxes in the prices
we paid our suppliers

SHARE OWNERS GOT 2.8¢ IN DIVIDENDS
($21 million)

3.1¢ WAS RE-INVESTED
($24 million) for a
better and more
secure future
for us all

OUTSIDE SUPPLIERS GOT 42.6¢
($332 million).. out of which
they had to pay their vendors,
employees, suppliers and
tax collectors

DISTRIBUTED AMONG
252,000
SHARE OWNERS
AS PAY FOR THE WORK
THEIR SAVINGS DO

The "Balanced Best Interests" of *All*

GENERAL ELECTRIC received $777,819,000 from customers for products and services during the first three months of 1953.

This total amount was distributed to the various claimants as shown above.

After all the other claims were met, the total profit remaining was 5.9¢ out of each dollar of sales.

* *All amounts stated in nearest millions of dollars.*

EMPLOYEE AND PLANT COMMUNITY RELATIONS

GENERAL 〖GE〗 ELECTRIC

(Specimen illustration from employee publication)

know what was the right thing to do in the balanced-best-interests of all concerned, but also had to discipline ourselves surely to do the right thing voluntarily when neither a policeman nor anyone else was looking.

Such moral concept and practice were going to be necessary for each individual contributor-claimant if he was to do his part in counteracting the charge that the many were being exploited for the benefit of the few. General Electric was not a toe-to-toe struggle between an employee "class" and an owner "class." It was a sort of clearinghouse where people came together to do things for each other. There were not different people in each of the five roles. They were largely the same. Many were in all five. Probably three fourths were in the four roles of employee, customer, neighboring citizen, and GE shareowner or direct or indirect owner in a supplier or dealer or member of a family benefiting from working for a supplier or dealer. Practically every contributor-claimant was in three roles at once. They simply turned their hats around pretty fast. We were thus rarely ever dealing with a narrow individual with only one specialized interest. But in the case of each, as has been indicated, there was great need to help him open his eyes to this fact. If, for instance, he had been wrongly persuaded to look at himself as only a worker, and to forget he was also a consumer and owner of property, he was likely to be a pushover for the demagogue who was trying to persuade him that he was not faring properly from voluntary private business and the other voluntary processes of the free economy, and that he should, therefore, turn to the destructive force sanctioned by a misled public opinion and winked at by the law-enforcement agencies of such a public's government. So, to avoid destructive action against his own interest later, each and every contributor-claimant needed to be informed earlier and kept reminded of where the common interest lay and why it was of value to the individual—economically and morally—to serve that common interest.

10 COMMUNITY RELATIONS

But if our employee went home to his family and neighbors with the beginnings of new knowledge as to his own interests and the beginnings of a new and favorable regard for General Electric's intentions, practices, and results, while a majority of his five to 50 neighbors had not yet acquired like beginnings, he would be quickly ridiculed out of any such budding ideas and might well cease to pay any attention to the help we were trying to offer him.

So it was obvious from the start that we would have to try to help surround our employee away from work—and not just at work—with influences to assist him in correcting any residue of past misinformation and in guarding against being actuated contrary to his interests by any new misinformation or unwarranted charges. The five to 50 neighbors per employee—adding up to as many as 50 thousand in a community where we had a thousand employees—had to be offered the same initial and corrective information as was offered to the employee. There were two reasons for this. The first was the resulting helpful effect of the neighbors on the employee as an employee. The other was its effect on the employee and his neighbors in their other contributor-claimant roles. And this would be no small job, for it was already evident that the influences against people cooperating with us and other businesses were much more varied, much more intense, and much more effective with the contributor-claimants outside than with the employees when at work.

We bought full-page advertising space in the plant-city newspapers to repeat for the neighbors there what we had told our employees about the nine-point job. We did the same to repeat our discussions of how big our profits were and whether they were too big. There were many other such ads.

We distributed the Guide to various thought-leaders in the communities. As already indicated, we developed an extensive distribution of the weekly *Employee Relations News Letter* to local editors, clergymen, teachers, businessmen, public servants, and others; the 4½-hour DuPont course, "How Our Business System Operates," was conducted for all our neighbors who wished it, and we trained other discussion leaders in this for those who wanted to carry on; and we used Professor Haney's text, "How You Really Earn Your Living," together with the other corrective materials we issued, as the basis for study and discussion groups not only at work but in the communities. Our managers and other thought-leaders were encouraged to start and run such groups not only for the direct good this would do among all the participants but also for the help it would give the leaders themselves both in packaging their new knowledge in ever more usable form and in developing their further facility in summoning up instantly the arguments and semantics needed to meet each public or private persuasion task in the face of ideological competitors who would otherwise be damagingly effective.

Because of our failure for so long to help employees and neighbors keep aware of how the individual and common interest was served by cooperation with rather than resistance to private business, the job for corrective thought-leaders in the communities had become enormous. The citizen at every level of intelligence and information tended to do his own thinking only up to a point, and then to depend for the rest on his thought-leader—who, in turn, could only go so far himself before calling on his thought-leader, and so on.

It seemed there was a thought-leader for every 8, or 10, or 12 people whether these people made up a baseball team, a football team, an army squad, a company president and his top officers, a U. S. President and his cabinet, or a little group in the corner of a shop or office or community.

The accompanying illustration is by no means exact. It is out of scale and a thing of this kind could not be definite in any event, since leaders will have varying spans of influence and many citizens listen to several thought-leaders. However, it is offered below to suggest something of the magnitude of the problem of equipping the thought-leaders in a community of 100,000 adults.

1

10

100

1,000

10,000

100,000 Adult Population

11,111 Thought-Leaders

These thought-leaders were in place in our plants and communities, but the vast majority of them were leading in the wrong direction. This needed to be changed so that just the opposite was true by converting all the current thought-leaders who could be straightened out and then helping to develop new ones who would replace these who could not be salvaged. Meanwhile, all digestible corrective education possible had to be offered directly to the nonleaders.

This local community job, like the internal employee job, was the responsibility of every manager in connection with all the citizens who came within his span of contacts or could be reached by him by other means.

11 MANAGERIAL COMPETENCY

For most of us managers, this new and expanded concept of our jobs meant that we would practically have to master and use a whole new profession while we kept on with our old one. We needed more knowledge than we had. We needed more time than we thought we had. We needed to show we were investing more heart-interest than we had so far made clear we entertained for our employees and neighbors.

But we could no longer ignore the vital importance of measuring up to the now-obvious requirements. We simply had to find a way. We had to go back to school, literally and figuratively, in order to acquire the needed new knowledge and the needed new skills in the application of that knowledge. We had to reorganize our prior working and thinking time—by delegating the more routine, more familiar, or less important work—in order to make room for the new study and the new skill development. We had to pay new attention to the way we thought, looked, acted, and spoke, on and off the job, to the end of being sure that our employees and neighbors judged and felt that our interest in them and intentions toward them were not only genuinely friendly in the best sense but were also far more than just materially motivated.

We were obviously facing a revolutionary change in what the typical manager in and out of General Electric had assumed was the extent of his personal responsibility and the field of his proper personal activity. Transcripts of my speeches in and out of the company contain this characteristic paragraph:

"I am more convinced every day that history is going to deal very harshly with me and most of my contemporaries—and with great justice—for our neglecting for so long our obvious responsibilities over and beyond the things we have been doing. We have gone along for half a century still fancying we were doing our full duty at our work when there was compelling evidence all around us that we were neglecting those additional kinds of work that we needed to do; we were blindly following our predecessors in doing what I impolitely call the 'mental cutting and paper shuffling' part of our job as though it were the whole job; we didn't even sense that the content of the managerial job of each of us was changing and expanding in new directions in a way that imposed urgent new requirements on us.

"This is not to overlook the very obvious fact that the objectives, diligence, manners and results of business in the public interest have all shown great progress. But in a country as wonderful as this—as is true maybe anywhere—our obligations are every bit as great as our opportunities. And my complaint about myself and my fellow participants in business is that our opportunities to serve the common good are so vast that what we are achieving is just not an acceptable percentage of what we should be finding ways to accomplish."

In the face of the newly recognized requirements, we set about to do our best to revolutionize—first in employee relations—our competency, activity, and results in these three very important areas in particular:

1. Good Human Interest—Both Ways

We simply had to be very sure that, to the extent humanly possible, we were doing right voluntarily and sincerely in the area of human association. We had to be sure, as we wanted to be—no matter what might be any human failings of the moment—not only that our intentions were the best and our performances improving but also that our efforts were being recognized for what they were.

Our employee did not live by bread alone. He did not work for bread alone. He would not and could not do his work well if he thought his return for it was to be in bread alone.

He wanted—and we wanted to give him—a boss who was on his side, who kept the human considerations up front in their very personal association, who respected and protected employee dignity, who engaged in genuine and forthright two-way, fully adequate, man-to-man communication on the things that to the employee's way of thinking counted.

He wanted—and we wanted to give him—a boss who provided him with a deserved sense of importance, significance, and genuine participation and who had a real interest in the employee both as a person and as a welcome and appreciated associate in the rewarding activity they were carrying on together.

The fellow we had been calling "boss" had to become recognized, welcomed, and believed as a teacher, leader, and salesman in previously undiscussed matters. The manager at every level had to depend to the last possible degree on getting things done right by getting his employees to know what was the right way and to want to do things that way.

In fact, any group of trainees in foremanship, in office management, or in engineering management who would not be about as acceptable for training as sales-engineers for the product of that plant no longer belonged in the supervisory training group as future suppliers of genuine job satisfaction.

Our employee would, in turn, have to look with seeing eyes at what was now going on—would have to discard his prior misconceptions and sober his emotions—so that he could maintain a determination to try to do right himself—and to want to do so—in this human relationship. He would obviously have to do his part to make it a rewarding two-way street.

Such a two-way human relationship could not be accomplished by superficial or spurious back-slapping or baby-kissing, or by sheer force of personality. It had to be based on a sound, deep, and deserved impression that both parties intended to do right in cooperating toward their common human ends, and were not just trying to "get away" with what appeared to be right. It had to be based on both parties doing their best to be right by applying the proper ideas and measures in trying to determine what was right in the circumstances.

A sufficiently earnest search by both for the facts would almost surely result in a common set of ideas, values, and even affections. And then the looks, words, and actions of both—even their silence—would make up the story.

What we needed was a vast and unfamiliar job of two-way communication—man-to-man communication, mass communication, formal and informal surveys, and other techniques—to get and exchange facts, to achieve understanding, to resolve misunderstandings and doubts, to pursue programs, and otherwise to implement and measure the progress we were all seeking in the human, moral, and emotional forces and satisfactions.

But history warned that this was not going to be nearly enough—in fact, by itself it would be practically useless. Much good work had been done in General Electric in this area—and all sorts of enlightened and constructive efforts had been made by hundreds of other companies—but it had nearly always wound up being almost or completely ineffective. The reason was that only the brute charge was treated; if the employer failed to meet the crook and exploiter charge adequately and convincingly, the employees were left to view their employer as, at best, simply the best of a bad lot and, at worst, as a real villain trying to "butter them up" with kind treatment in order to soften them up for the easier or even unnoticed picking of their pockets by the employer.

2. Good Economic Understanding—Both Ways

So, as the next and absolutely necessary requirement for reaching our goal of employee satisfaction and cooperation, we saw it as imperative that we in top management, as well as all our other managers, (1) understand, and then (2) teach, where jobs come from, how free people act in a free market, how we all work for each other as interdependent specialists in General Electric's subdivided operations, and how in general our business and economic system operates.

We had to learn and teach the facts about money and inflation; about taxes; about private enterprise as differentiated from collectivist systems; about the value of incentives, savings, technology, risk, competition, profit and loss, and other returns varying with performance; about war booms and readjustments.

We felt it would be helpful for us to show employees and the rest of the public what money comes into the business and how much of it goes to suppliers, to taxes, to employees, to reinvestment in growth and strength, and to shareowners in dividends.

We were sure our employee could not possibly know whether we were being fair with him—and not short-changing or exploiting him—unless he appreciated that there were two kinds of work done in a business: one kind by the minds and muscles of managers and other employees and the other kind by people's savings risked in designs, in arm-lengthening facilities, in inventory, in customer accounts, and the like. Employees would also have to appreciate that both kinds of work quite properly had to be paid for at the market price or they would not get done and there would soon be no jobs.

Some socialist enemies—who did not approve of the private business system at all—were loudly and scornfully claiming that they knew more about our individual businesses and our economic system than management did. And too many people believed them—with what justice the reader may decide for himself.

In any event, a startling change in managerial competence and activity was considered the most important and necessary one to be accomplished—and the hardest one to accomplish. A more thorough understanding of job economics, and also of private business economics overall—together with an almost totally new facility in making ourselves understood and convincing in this area—was vitally needed not only in employee relations but also in all the other relations areas of General Electric.

We were sure this acquisition would give us the courage—of which we had had too little in the past—to speak up boldly and confidently with facts and considered opinions which would be helpful to employees and neighbors, no matter how unwelcome and unpalatable it might be at first to those very ones in whose interests we were working and whose respect and friendship we sought, and no matter who had to be contradicted meanwhile among those of good or evil power.

Where we had knowledge of our employees being misled about something-for-nothing or misled otherwise with misinformation that might lead them to act against their own interests in areas of our association, there was no escape from our being a party to their deception and self-injury if we did not try to provide our employees with the corrective information. As Henri Frederick Amiel put it:

"Truth is not only violated by falsehood; it may be equally outraged by silence."

We businessmen had been running our businesses exactly the way our worst detractors wanted them run. In no area had this

Who Is Telling The Truth
—And Who Isn't?

WHOSE PROMISES
WERE KEPT?
—and Whose Charges Were Wrong?

We Withdraw
A Statement...

We Start the New Year
with This Resolution...

In 1949, we are going to try to be a better employer. We are going to try to have General Electric an even better place to work.

Last year General Electric foremen and other supervisors—all management in fact—spent more time than ever before in Company history studying how to do their jobs better; how to be better leaders; how to get along better with the people who daily work with them; how to be more considerate, more helpful, more responsive to the needs, wishes and feelings of their employees in the conduct of the day's work.

This year we are resolved to intensify our efforts to put into practice what we have learned from our past successes and our failures, to become a better employer and to make General Electric a better place to work, by doing everything in our power to put the human considerations first.

(Excerpts from articles in employee publications)

been so true as in our silence in the face of false charges about our honest intentions and fruitful results. In this area, as in no other, history will surely ridicule any claims of ours to alertness, wisdom, resourcefulness, and courage.

Happily, from the very start of our efforts, there was immediate and ample encouragement to the hope that our employees wanted to depend on, and be on the side of, a stout and honest leader who told the unpleasant truth as he saw it when under fire.

It had been obvious that employees and others were getting suspicious of the business executive who, despite his known convictions to the contrary, always said what he thought his listeners wanted to hear, and who showed outward approval for people and ideas he was known to condemn rather violently in the privacy and safety of his panelled office. The hard fact was that, while business executives had long been expected to be leaders, there had never in history been an instance where people had confidence in a wobbly or frightened leader.

Obviously this two-way job-economics education process was going to be a two-way study and a two-way discussion project of no mean proportions.

But even it—plus the human relations program—was not going to be enough. The facts would have to be nailed down so they would not come loose.

3. Good Sophistication—Both Ways

At this point, sound guidance from successful consumer marketing had to be relied on again. In nearly every sale, after the positive story is in as to what the product will do for the buyer and as to why it will do more than will competitors' offerings, the time comes when any residual objections to buying have to be removed from the customer's mind.

Incidentally, as many readers will already know, the final part in any good sales training course—and usually the hardest part for the salesman to master—is that called "overcoming objections." The first requirement, of course, is a top-quality product offered at the proper market price. But that is far from enough. Also required is that the salesman have a thorough knowledge of his product and of the products of competition; that he be sensitive to an individual's human values and human reactions; that he be able to express himself clearly and agreeably; and that he be able to win the confidence of the buyer in himself as well as his product.

Some of the customer's objections may come from a prior habit of mind or from a competitor's perfectly honest but more thorough or personable salesmanship; both of which must be met and removed by further facts, or by the more persuasive repetition of facts already presented.

But some of the resistance—and, at times, all of it—will come from product misinformation and emotional prejudice wittingly or unwittingly supplied by competitors of evil or good intent. Removing such resistance is a delicate job of forthright correction of the misinformation and of careful overcoming of the emotional prejudice. What has to be shown in the end—as kindly and humbly as humanly possible—is that the competitors are either ignorant or liars. A hasty or an insufficiently thoughtful tyro will stir more prejudice and resistance than he cures when he starts disillusioning a customer about a previously trusted informant.

As the requirement of honesty on the part of the salesman has come up, it may be of interest to some readers to know how this was handled back in my time as a trainer of door-to-door washing machine salesmen. A considerable percentage of these budding geniuses always seemed to join the classes with the idea they were going to learn something pretty slick. In connection with admonitions to become familiar with the product and faithfully state what it would do for the housewife, someone would almost invariably ask a question which boiled down to, "What is the salesman's allowable ratio of exaggeration?" After much discussion, those still feeling some exaggeration was necessary to the sale would finally come down to deciding that the salesman was allowed whatever exaggeration would be equal to the discount the prospective buyer was putting on what she was being told. Further discussion would then bring out that the salesman in such a case was admittedly and intentionally lying and that—even though the housewife bought the machine and found it to be what she had guessed it was going to be rather than what the salesman had promised it would be—she would know the salesman had lied to her. She would then be all too likely to let the machine be repossessed and to refuse to buy his next offering, such as a refrigerator. Meanwhile, she would spread the word far and wide among friends and neighbors that the salesman and his machines were not to be trusted. Satisfied users, who were a principal influence in a salesman's sales and commissions, were those who discovered they had been told the truth. So—however reluctantly on the part of those who had been leaning toward exaggeration in the beginning—the whole class finally would come to the inescapable conclusion that the salesman's allowable ratio of exaggeration was zero. Repeat sales depended on the truth, and even where he failed on the first try, the truthful salesman could come back for a second try whereas the liar could not.

In one way or another this fact is taught by all companies— and employed by all salesmen—who win and maintain the confidence of their customers. Truth in selling is a fact of life in a private business that succeeds and long survives.

In the field of ideological competition between something-for-something and something-for-nothing advocates, we were sure, truth would prove to be just as powerful, and misrepresentation just as devastating, once our contributor-claimant had access to the facts and time to digest them unemotionally. The bold and truthful salesman of a good product in this job field—as in any other—could hope for no greater windfall than to have as a competitor a lying salesman who made big false charges and big false promises on neither of which he could make good and which would be so much the easier to debunk because of the ridiculously wide margin between the false claims and the demonstrable truth. Nevertheless, the crooked or misguided salesman in the ideological field would too often be persuasive because he appealed to wishful thinking and employed deceptive side-of-the-angels semantics. It would often become necessary to show not only that he was wrong but also that his misrepresentations were selfishly moti-vated and were contrary to the real interests of those he was professing to serve. Too many managers tended to be trusting souls, and too often belonged to the "Little Bo Peep" school of sophistication, as a result of having spent so much of their time with business people whose word was good and whose intentions were honorable. The attainment of the required degree of sophistication himself—and then acquiring and employing a facility for imparting this sophistication to his employees in job-connected matters—was going to be a rough, demanding, and sometimes quite unpleasant job for the individual manager at every level.

One of our directors had told us that the "competent business manager" had to have these skills and characteristics:

1. The ability to work effectively with people.
2. The ability to make sound decisions in the light of available facts and under pressure of time.
3. The ability to draw upon a fund of substantive knowledge and upon the capacities of others who possessed specialized skills and knowledge.
4. The capacity to draw these abilities together and use them as an integrated whole.

But I hope I have made clear my conviction that, in working with people, making decisions, and getting them well carried out, the constructive manager cannot be simply a census taker, a consolidater, a coordinator, a follower, a typical politician. He is in a political position, all right, and he should cater as much as possible to the likes, dislikes, and wishes of his constituents: his contributor-claimants. But the time comes when he has done all that he reasonably can in that direction and must try to change their likes, dislikes, and wishes—that is, must try to change what is "good politics" with them—in order to serve their own best interests.

Not all—and maybe not even a majority—of the hundreds of thousands of contributor-claimants could be expected to take the time, or even then to be able, to understand the soundness of the information and conclusions offered toward such constructive change in their ideas and wishes. The decisive factor would be General Electric's credibility—specifically, how many would give us the benefit of the doubt about what they did not yet understand. There were easily 20,000 of us who were in positions of managerial and professional responsibility and who thus, by our every word, act, and even look, "spoke" in one way or another for General Electric both on and off the job. It was necessary that the

THE INITIALS OF A FRIEND

We want **YOU** to have
YOUR share

(Specimen headlines from articles in employee publications)

overwhelming majority be convincing in privately and publicly carrying out the Company mission to such degree that any thoughtless or disobedient departure from policy by a few would be recognized as that inevitable exception unfortunately to be expected in human affairs.

No manager could possibly meet the new requirements completely. However, there was encouragement from the very beginning that the vast majority would try—with varying devotion and, of course, with varying results. The important thing was that we were at last trying in previously neglected fields.

12 THE MANAGER'S OWN NINE-POINT JOB

Before leaving the subject of the needed changes in managerial equipment and practices, we should mention a very important early development.

As already noted, I had disobeyed my initial instructions just once. I had gone to see an industrial relations vice-president who, incidentally, later became the chief executive of his great company. He had asked what was the scope of my staff responsibilities on the new job—and particularly whether I had staff responsibility for exempt salaries clear up to the top. Upon being told I did not, he said flatly that I had better get it or the program would not work down through the various levels necessary. I knew such an increase in my responsibilities was impossible at the moment, so I did not pay enough attention to the reasons he gave and promptly forgot the whole thing in the press of other matters.

But his reasons were suddenly recalled when we began to witness what was happening. The foreman, in particular, had seemed to welcome the promised new program in the hope that it would be helpful in his area of responsibility, where, of course, the resistance to cooperation was the most evident although not necessarily the most costly. But his enthusiasm to equip himself and help his employees was being dampened or cancelled out by a lack of evidence that he was going to get from his supervisor the nine-point job he was trying to provide for his employees. His supervisor showed no sign of any thirst for new knowledge or for anything approaching a regeneration of the spirit; he seemed still to be a tough and even stingy boss with no sign of wanting to become a salesman of an excellently remodeled product. Also, when this supervisor, in turn, looked over his shoulder at his superintendent or vice-president, he didn't think he detected any sign of "rebirth" in the latter.

As a result, managers and others in the exempt salary group were putting more credence than even the nonexempt employees were in the loud claims by our detractors that this supposed new program was just a hoax engineered by an evil "propagandist brought in from Madison Avenue" to wring some extra profits out of the employees until the falsity of the promises later came to light.

There was, of course, valid dissatisfaction with the low levels of pay in the exempt salary field not only at General Electric but elsewhere as well. There were two reasons for these low levels.

One was the heavy concentration of attention and scarce resources on just keeping plants open and providing some work and pay for the lower-skilled employees, who had had the toughest time during the long depression. I had had a vivid and even wryly amusing demonstration of this on a visit with my boss to a General Electric plant at the depth of the depression and a good 13 years before I joined the company. I had been lucky enough to have had only one 10 percent pay cut by then, but at General Electric such cuts, even despite promotions, were becoming commonplace and were no joking matter. For instance, one old timer then in the upper-responsibility range told afterwards of having four important increases in his duties between 1931 and 1937, along with five cuts in pay totalling 28½ percent. Had we known this, we should not have been so surprised at what happened in the office of the gentleman whom we were seeing and whose promotion to vice president had just been announced that morning. An old friend opened the door without knocking, poked his head in, and inquired: "Is it so?" The answer was a modest, "Well, yes, I guess so." Whereupon his friend exclaimed: "Gosh, that's too bad! How much did they dock you?"

The other cause had been the more recent practice in the World War II and postwar labor market of raising pay by the same flat cents per hour for all wage earners and by a like amount expressed in dollars per week or month for the salaried employees. Not only had this kept salaries at far too low levels and narrowed still further the already too small or even nonexistent differentials between hourly and salaried pay; it also had further narrowed the all-important differentials between grades within the salary structure.

The obvious violence to incentive and equity from these two causes had long been accepted with good grace as an appropriate sacrifice in good cause but, at the same time, as something the need for which would soon pass. But when it continued into and beyond the Korean period—in the face of rising market prices of managerial, professional, and other skills in the exempt group—General Electric began to lose some important people, and the enthusiasm of many others declined sharply.

How much this neglect had become an ingrained habit was demonstrated by an incident that occurred after our new program was well under way. Following a top management meeting on the necessity of getting the nine-point job in effect at each management level before expecting it to be put in place at the next level down, an officer immediately called in his ranking subordinate, who also was an officer and with whom he had travelled about the country for years discussing everything freely except, apparently, the all-important question of the subordinate's pay. Upon being asked point blank, "How do you like your pay?," the startled subordinate jumped up, leaned solicitously over his boss's desk, and said almost in a whisper, "Are you well?"

A few more such specific soundings, on top of the obvious general evidence of need, prompted one of the most comprehensive and thorough market price studies ever made in so specialized and sensitive an area. This resulted in a whole new salary structure which removed the distortions produced in this area by the years of difficulty and neglect; it raised salaries for the various grades to the market levels and provided a range within each grade for varying merit, thus providing not only a real incentive for excellence within each grade but also an even stronger incentive for that further excellence that would warrant promotion to the next.

Incidentally, adopting the going market price at each salary level was all that was needed to restore those between-grades differentials that were proper and workable from the standpoint of equity and incentive.

The result was enthusiastically received for itself, and the recipients also took it as evidence that the rest of their own nine-point jobs would at least be forthcoming.

But we had to realize that the result would not remain acceptable—and, more important, would not remain equitable and workable as among the various contributor-claimants—unless our government stopped cheapening its money to please some people and to fool the vast remainder of its citizens. The new salary program was based on the effective efforts the market had made to correct the inadequate differentials between the participants in what was a distorted and not a free market—something the market always attempts to do after any distortion. But the whole pay structure had been pushed way up not by the free market but by the arbitrary force of government action to cause inflation and thus to mask the mistaken actions of its own and those of its supporters whose demands it was politically inadvisable to deny.

If the inflation continued, the market would have to keep trying to work out the successive restoration of the proper relationships among the contributor-claimants. And while I for one did not approve of the inflationary course the government was pursuing, certainly all of us at General Electric were determined to see that our employees, salaried as well as hourly, had their pay kept up to what was right and appropriate in relation to what similar skills and performance were commanding in that market.

In connection with this subject of inflation, I welcomed the occasional visits of a prominent university's much publicised economist whom I had known since youth. He would drop in the office or see me after hours and would good-humoredly give me a going-over on the less-fashionable of my views in so-called "labor economics." I would charge him with having fallen for the something-for-nothing school of economics, and he would try to show me how out of step with the times I was—although he never went quite as far as my most prized critic, who claimed I was "to the right of Marie Antoinette."

Nevertheless, we had no real difficulty in agreeing, despite our differing viewpoints, that above-the-market pay increases forced on employers were technically and actually not the "inflationary" pay increases which they were being too generally called by businessmen, editors, professors, and others, and that, also, they were not taken primarily out of profits, as the public was being led to believe, but were almost entirely at the expense of workers or consumers or both; for these increases would simply cause unemployment when the employer tried to recover the artificially higher costs by raising prices unless the government had meanwhile rushed to cheapen money further in order to mask or delay or reduce temporarily the job-killing effect of the increases; that, in short, it was not by itself what the unions and government did, in raising the price of labor above the market, which caused the inflation, but this combined with the action of government officials in cheapening the value of our money.

What we could never agree on—and could not even come up with definite separate views on—was how much time it took for a pattern-setting increase by a conspicuous employer to spread across the work force, how far it finally spread, how many were left out for a time or entirely, and therefore how much of an underserved advantage the relatively few employees who kept working in the initial company or industry had over the balance of the work force in that industry or elsewhere who faced the higher prices but were laid off or had to wait a month or a year or two years for the "catch-up" increase.

Another thing we discussed on several occasions over the years was a feeling I had that these successive increases, especially in the unskilled and lower-skilled areas, not only were causing unemployment needlessly but also were forcing investment in faster mechanization than was economic. And as union actions, minimum wage laws, or other influences caused these bottom pay rates to rise faster than the rates for the skills on up the scale, the market would of course go to work—union or no union—to iron out the inequities between contributor-claimants by reestablishing the workable differentials between skills, which inevitably resulted in raising all the upper rates. Thus the public was then standing the expense not only of the unemployment and of carrying the needless extra investment but also of the effect the extra increases in the lower rates had had in raising the whole rate structure.

A subject we kept coming back to more than any other was why it was the economics teachers had had so little success in teaching economics here in a country which had almost universal literacy and which depended for its survival on the ability of the majority of voters to make the right decisions in a succession of economic responsibilities decentralized to them. Washington, for example, seemed full of public servants—from conservatives to welfare-staters—who suffered at having to do so many economically foolish things because they judged their constituents would not understand if they did what was not foolish. I kept insisting that only a little honest economic explanation by government officials to the voters—confirmed by widespread public dissemination of the applicable facts in simple "country" words by my friend's economics-teaching fraternity in schools, universities, citizens meetings, and mass media—would result in quickly changing it from "bad politics" to "good politics" to collect government costs back in open, honest, visible taxes on the individual citizens instead of collecting these same costs from the same citizens surreptitiously through so-called "taxes on business" and through the brutal and regressive tax of inflation. I hope the present and future generations will find a better solution to economic education for the voting majority than my friend and I—or anybody in our generation—could come up with. As has been indicated in earlier chapters, we in General Electric were trying to have our managers and other thought-leaders learn and contribute as much as possible along this line because of its very vital job-connected relationship. And there was plenty of encouraging evidence that rewarding results would come from even rudimentary efforts.

In addition to being alert to changes in the salary market, our managers would have another problem that warranted their best attention continuously. That was the determination of merit and the prompt recognition of it. Naturally, in any such transaction where merit was the criterion, there would always be a residual difference of opinion depending on how observant, how in possession of the same common facts, how economically literate, how mutually trusting of one another, how realistic, and how unemotional the two parties to the transaction were. This made close attention and prompt action in this area all the more essential.

Despite the vigilance that would be required, the comprehensive initial adjustments—and the assurances of trying thereafter to keep their pay up to what was right and appropriate in all the circumstances—were warmly welcomed by the managers and were taken as evidence that the rest of their own nine-point jobs would be forthcoming and that each could in good conscience go to work to see that his five to 50 employees got their full nine-point jobs.

13 THE FIRST NEGOTIATIONS

As in the case of the salary structure, we had distortions in the wage structure both as to levels and as to differentials between grades. Both had come via the flat cents-per-hour increases already mentioned.

In contrast to the situation as to salaries, the wage levels—particularly in the lowest-skill areas—were much higher than any free-market action would have yielded. They had been forced there artificially by unions and government.

As to the differentials between grades, the situation was analogous to the salaried classifications. The flat increases had been the basic cause of the narrowing, and minimum-wage activities by government under union pressure had compounded the inequities. Walsh-Healey, Bacon-Davis, and other such influences were complicating factors. The higher up the skill and usefulness ladder an employee was, the greater was his quite understandable sense of injustice.

These were matters that would have to be handled in negotiations over the years with over 40 unions having over 100 separate contracts, and we would be able to have a very limited plus-or-minus range in which to work out any variations we believed to be more constructive than the practices generally prevailing in negotiated settlements.

For instance, we judged it to be obvious that each hourly and salaried job should be placed at the proper level and in the proper relationship to other jobs. Thereafter, any general adjustments should not be in flat dollars or cents but on a percentage basis so the proper relationships would be preserved and any justified complaints about inequities as to differentials would be minimized. But it took us five years to get this started in the face of the firmly established contrary practice.

The first negotiations under the new program were coming up in that spring of 1948, and we were intending as nearly as possible to be as constructive in this negotiated area, where our voluntary leeway was quite restricted, as we had been trying to be since the previous summer in the much broader fields still open to unrestricted direct activities toward good employee and community relations and cooperation.

We had had national and independent unions at our various plants from time to time. We had always dealt with them in accordance with our employees' wishes. When the new wave of unionization came along in the 1930s and one particular union had been certified in a number of our plants as our employees' choice, we had voluntarily entered into one of the first—if not the first—multiplant contracts in the country. This had proved to be a tremendous help to this and other unions in getting the similar multiplant contracts which they so desired at other large companies. As in the case of the others, we continued to deal with this union in good faith—as our employees evidently wished us to do and as the Federal Government kept ordering us in no uncertain terms to do—even after the suspicion had become widespread in and out of government that this union was Communist-dominated and after we had testified before Senate and House committees that we felt the government should stop certifying this union to us and other companies.

As an instance in point, the War Labor Board had reported in 1945 that "labor relations between company and union have been on an unusually sound and constructive level."

But all this past effort at working together properly, constructively, and, at times, even indulgently with the various unions certified to us—and the clear evidence of our more recent efforts to ferret out and cure any warranted dissatisfaction—had not seemed to cause gratitude or gratification on the part of most of the union officials involved or to stir a noticeable response in kind. While they generally conducted themselves quite temperately in personal contacts with us, most of their publications, hand bills, and news releases continued as before to attack us, like other employers, with emotion-charged defamation for which we usually could find little or no excuse. In fact, the national and local printed matter distributed by the more vocal unions at General

How Does General Electric Feel About Unions?

What Do You Ask of a Union?

...But Do Unions Need to be **This** Wrong?

Why Joe Wants Your Union

(Specimen headlines and illustration from employee publications)

Electric and that coming to my desk from the more vocal unions outside—regardless of whether they were or were not thought to be Communist-dominated—all seemed to read like the Communist "Daily Worker" in such matters as the attacks on managers and owners as brutes and crooks, the picturing of the private business system as an exploiter of the many for the benefit of the few, and the promotion of gang force rather than worth or willing exchange as the way for the individual to get what he wanted. This sounded like war for war's sake or, at least, like the classic "class struggle" at its rawest. And it was hard to avoid the impression that the particular spokesmen involved did not want to reform us in any way that would result in our working in peace with reasonably satisfied and cooperating employees; rather, what they seemed to me to want, and even to feel was necessary, was to keep the employees in such an emotional state that they would continue to be upset over fancied wrongs after any real ones had been corrected.

For a long time, too many of our managers had believed that all these public attacks on business went over the heads of our employees. And too many managers certainly believed that the specific attacks on General Electric were so inexcusably vicious and so obviously contrary to the evident facts of our good intentions, good treatment, and good jobs that our employees just couldn't be looking right at such good things and seeing them as bad. But we all had had quite a shock when, at plant after plant in 1946, union officials had proved they had a "push-button" control over employees and could cause them not only to strike on call but also, in too many cases, to do senseless and frightful damage to the investment in their places of work.

It is hard to look back now over the intervening years and realize the extent of the support which the union officials had commanded not only from the city administrations and police in the matter of very open and flagrant lawbreaking but also from merchants, teachers, students, press, clergy, and seemingly most of the other local thought-leaders as well as the rest of the neighbors.

As has already been indicated, the new program had had as its objective the deserving and thus the regaining of the favorable regard and the active cooperation of employees and neighbors in their own interests through—

1. Correcting any causes of justified employee and community dissatisfaction by getting them to tell us what was wrong and then doing all possible not only to right any such wrongs but also to try to right them their way and not ours.

2. Correcting any misinformation or misconceptions that caused unwarranted dissatisfaction—no matter how far afield we had to go in our own improved education and in helping our employees update their knowledge—and no matter who of high or low estate had to be contradicted in the process.

I for one had long felt that the theory underlying unionism was good, and that unions had served well in the early stages in the human-considerations area by forcibly alerting us managers to the need and desirability of abandoning sins of neglect on the one hand and paternalism on the other, and of developing instead a genuine two-way relationship that would prove rewarding in a human way. In the economic area, I was also ready to assume that some early good had been done, although, as previously indicated, my concern was mounting as to the influential role many union officials seemed to be playing in the promotion of inflation through government and in the misrepresentation of private business. It should also be stated that there seemed to be some evidence that many employees were coming to feel that they were more likely to be pushed around by the union steward than by the company foreman.

In the face of all this, we had no alternative but to continue to try to get through to all concerned the truth, as best we could determine it, as to where the common interest lay and why we were devoting our best efforts in that direction.

To test our intended conduct in the coming negotiations, we intended to examine our plans and procedures for dealing with our job-customers and their agents against the same experience and standards we would call on in dealing with our product-customers and their agents.

Unfortunately, we had been drifting along with the developing fashion of the times. We had been falling into the habit of making our bargaining offers on the low side, with the full and realistic expectation that we would be "traded up" step by step to the final settlement—often to the accompaniment of much questionable "news" reporting by union officers to employees and communities while we remained silent.

For instance, if everything pointed to a five-cent increase being about right, there was a strong tendency among employers in those days to offer nothing at first. Then, under public strike-threat pressure, about half would be offered. Then, after all the union representatives had been called in from the plants and the resulting vote for a strike had been well aired in a receptive press, management would "capitulate" by upping the offer to the full five cents per hour.

This, of course, played right into the hands of any union officials who felt a need for political reasons for a conspicuous "triumph over greedy and vicious management" by succeeding— with the aid of staunch "solidarity" of membership support—in "dragging the company unwillingly" to do the right thing by the employees.

While all this may have been recognized as amateur theatricals by any sophisticated bystander even when he knew he was affected, any tendency on our part to go along further with this fashion would be inexcusably misleading to our employees and neighbors. This would be an immoral and stupid effort to "cooperate" with others in fooling the very people those trust we were seeking to deserve and get. We could no longer be silent about our good intentions and sound accomplishments—nor about false charges against us which might lead employees and neighbors to act contrary to their interests in the areas of our mutual concern. Incidentally, if a product competitor had been so indiscreet and untruthful as to level such unwarranted charges against our product offerings and our moral character, he would have been promptly excoriated in the public press and dragged through all the available courts in embarrassing and expensive law suits. Yet it was the fashion of the times for employers to act unnaturally by remaining silent in the face of untrue union charges—and thus appear to confess guilt. One professor in a leading graduate business school even pled with me to stop my corrective communications on the ground that the cause of the particular union official he was discussing was so just he should be permitted some misrepresentation!

We believed that union officials representing our employees should have every bit of credit for every good thing they did. But we also believed they should have a sounder and nobler function to perform than fooling their members. While it was not the basic reason for our wanting to tell the truth and not become untruthful by remaining silent, we were presumptuous and hopeful enough to believe we could help the union officials by telling the facts in a way that would make it "good politics" with their members for them to settle down at the bargaining table in a more constructive common quest for what was in the balanced-best-interests of all concerned.

In any event, we were through with any behavior—however fashionable or expedient—that would intentionally mislead our employees and neighbors either about the union officials or about us. And if we did not stick religiously to this determination, we would not be acting with that single standard of research, preparation, value, full information, and courageous forthrightness which had made our product customer relations so materially successful and so humanly rewarding.

To serve the interests of employees and all others, there was nothing for all concerned to do but try to arrive at what was right for all. No one should even consider attempting to get the better of another contributor-claimant in a situation where both economics and honor dictated that each try his level best to see that each got no more and no less than was rightly coming to him, for that was the arrangement that would provide the best, most, and steadiest jobs to employees and supply the most rewarding returns to the neighbors.

We intensified our research for facts likely to be pertinent in the coming negotiations. We particularly sifted all the job-market information we could get from all sources, including union publications, news releases, and interviews with union officials.

We then added to, discarded, or revised this information on the basis of the formal union demands and any additional or different facts we learned from union and other sources during the many days of meetings at the bargaining table and elsewhere that made up the negotiating process.

Then, when it finally seemed evident that all the individual items of current interest, together with all the available related information of real significance, had been fully considered and discussed to the point of exhausting all the possibilities, we made a comprehensive and complete offer. This offer was made up of that combination of gives and takes—that combination of eliminations, continuances, and additions—which would constitute the appropriate "new model" job at what the market indicated was the right market price in pay and benefits.

Keep in mind that this offer was no invention of ours out of the blue, and no surprise sprung on the union officials at the start of negotiations. It represented no slavish or rigid adherence to any preconceived fixed position, and we would be concerned with no such archaic and silly fear as wounded pride or loss of face if we changed it. Both sides, as usual, had come to the bargaining table a lot closer than the overblown original demands and attendant publicity might have suggested. We had been trying there to exhaust every possibility of modifying our previous estimates—and any actual ones of the union officials—in the direction of what would better actuate and reward all the contributor-claimants. To be sure, such help as we received from the union officials in arriving at the sound ingredients of an equitable settlement not only was far less than we would have welcomed but was hard to come by at all. The union officials would keep on publicly repeating their completely unrealistic demands seemingly because, besides hoping for some further "splitting of the difference" under later circumstances, they also felt a vested interest in creating and prolonging dissatisfaction, not in curing it.

The offer we finally made was merely an assembly of long-familiar elements, each of which had been as appropriately modified or as exhaustively considered in the many days of two-way bargaining-table discussion as seemed necessary. Formal or informal agreement had already been reached on many elements. As to others, there was general understanding amounting to tacit recognition even though actual agreement had been quite understandably withheld by the union negotiators because of residual objections, because they were waiting to see what would be forthcoming as to the other elements, or because of tactical plans for calling in third parties on the chance there would be "splitting of the difference."

The offer was as fully in the balanced-best-interests of all as it was humanly possible for us to make it at the moment. It represented private business management acting naturally in the best sense of that word—for it reflected the full truth as we saw it, with nothing held back for spurious jockeying of the type earlier described or for any out-moded haggling of the "flea-bitten eastern bazaar" type. This was too serious a matter—involving the welfare of many hundreds of thousands of people—to be treated as a cheap political opportunity or handled with silly or insincere heroics.

A union contract was then, as it is now, largely a collection of concessions by the employer; there was little or nothing of importance the union was to do; and in any case contracts had come more and more to be enforceable against employers only. One of the most incredible aberrations that had developed in this field was the successful refusal by unions to cancel or even reduce any prior employer concession, however impracticable it had subsequently proved to be in the working-conditions area or in piece rates or elsewhere. We were sure this was wrong in principle—as well as so visibly and inevitably wrong in practice— and certainly contrary to the balanced interests of the contributor-claimants. We felt we had an obligation to try to rectify a mistake as soon as it proved to be such. If we did not try, we would be a party to perpetuating our own worst mistakes or the worst mistakes of others who might have been the "pattern setters" willingly or under pressure they could not withstand.

For instance, one of the eliminations in the new-model offer was the "maintenance of membership" which had been imposed on the members under wartime pressure of unions and government. This was very popular with the union officials but not with those employees who were forced to pay dues unwillingly and might not have approved of the union. We felt this had been an unwarranted invasion of the individual employee's freedom of choice. This elimination was equivalent to our taking out of a former consumer deal a legal fee which the consumer's lawyer wanted us to collect in the price and pay to him but which the consumer thought was excessive or altogether unnecessary.

This was our best effort to copy the kind of diligent and able product planning and pricing which General Electric and other alert companies had used with success for years in pleasing people in consumer-product marketing. As a result of the "prior homework" done over the required period, the product was sent to market with a fair degree of certainty that it not only would meet the consumers' basic and extra satisfaction demands but also would prove to be attractively priced. The process had become relatively foolproof, as was demonstrated by the hundreds of thousands of new or improved products which came to market each year and which, in "that plebiscite of the market place," were bought by "the voters" in about the volume expected and at the predetermined prices.

However, despite the reliability of the system itself, even such highly placed and paid human beings as the marketing managers would inevitably make the occasional human error in the market information reported back to the product- and price-planning sessions. Incidentally, such mistakes, when acted on, generally proved to be so horribly expensive as to permit no repetition that could be avoided, so the erring marketing manager was likely to find himself stripped of his job and company limousine and back selling brushes or nylons door-to-door on commission.

While duplicating in job-marketing this process developed in consumer marketing might seem at first glance to be too tough to try, there were some factors which made the procedure actually simpler and more predictable. For example, the risk that the market situation would change in the intervening time did not have to be taken, and the representatives of the job-customers were right at hand to help up to the moment of decision on the most appropriate offer to be made for the immediate market.

Nevertheless, in view of the ever-present possibility of human error—and keeping in mind our deep conviction at General Electric that we can't stay big unless we are humble—we assured the union officials in 1948, as we told all concerned in connection with all further offers over the succeeding 13 years, that, while our offer represented the best information we had at the moment as to what the offer should be, we would be not only willing but eager to change it instantly on getting any old or new information proving that change would be in the balanced-best-interests of all. We emphasized that no false pride in the offer and no silly face-saving about changing it would deter us in the slightest from embracing any improvements that would make the offer still more workable for all the cooperating contributor-claimants. We added that no strike or strike threat would be classed as the kind of evidence that indicated the offer should be changed.

We also told the union negotiators that—to help them and us to be sure that their members and our other employees and neighbors understood the many features and details of the offer—we were taking full-page advertising space that evening in all the plant city newspapers to report the full text of the offer exactly as we had given it to them in printed form for discussion in that morning's bargaining sessions.

After having time to study the quite long document, the officers of the largest union returned in a day or so to say they would accept the offer as tendered. Other unions followed. Incidentally, this was the first and only time in my 14 years on the job that any union accepted such an initial all-inclusive offer. All subsequent ones were revised in major or minor ways.

The features and extent of the new-model job were welcomed by the employees, and both the employees and their families and neighbors were relieved at having been subjected to no strike call and to none of the usual "crisis" build-up.

The union sector was silent for the moment.

14 PERSPECTIVE

Before going into the aftermath of these first negotiations under the new overall program of employee and community relations, and before giving the rest of the necessarily voluminous report on the union-related part of our activities, a caution as to perspective seems worthwhile.

To repeat, the objective of the new program was to deserve and win the cooperation of the employees and neighbors in their own interests—which, incidentally, would also be in the balanced interests of all the contributor-claimants.

Out at the plant operations, 95 percent or more of the typical supervisor's time at any level was spent in helping his five to 50 employees be more productive and want to be so. If local negotiations and other union-connected activities averaged 5 percent of his time, it would be remarkable—even though he included the time spent in countering union-sponsored appeals to the employees not to cooperate toward what we believed to be the good ends of the business. For, out at the local level, the direct union-sponsored influence against cooperation—as conveyed by stewards, publications, and news releases—was not nearly so great as was, unfortunately, the influence toward noncooperation exerted by other national and local agencies of public opinion formation encountered in the local community.

And at our staff headquarters in New York a good 75 to 80 percent of our time and attention was likewise spent on the same kind of cooperation-inducing influences handled directly with the employees, with only the remainder spent on the actual union relations.

While I no longer have available a detailed description of our headquarters setup and duties at the end of negotiations in 1948, it was substantially the same as at the start of 1954, described below. This exact transcript of our report to our managers in the January 15, 1954, *Employee Relations News* only reminded our 15,000 managers and others of what I have said above about not confusing the volume of printed matter or publicity with the amount of attention and effort given to our employee and community relations activities in the permitted areas beyond negotiations or other matters which were directly union-connected.

January 15, 1954

TO OUR MANAGEMENT:

This letter tries normally, as you know, to report fact and opinion of the most urgent current importance to our operations.

In the process, an unfortunately large proportion of the space still has to be given to supplying the facts with which to correct the more flagrant misinformation being aimed by others at our employees and neighbors.

Viewed by itself, this publication might thus tend to obscure the full range of our daily activities and leave an unbalanced impression of our intentions and efforts.

So, as we all begin another New Year, it seems worthwhile to record here again the summary which we hope will help keep in proper perspective both the more and the less well-known ways in which we in your Employee and Plant Community Relations Services Division are trying to aid you in the attainment of our Company's objectives.

Some of our work, of course, is still made needlessly controversial by others. It is often considered "news" by current standards, and thus tends to be widely noted. But it is important to keep in mind that this involves only a small part of our work in one relatively narrow area among many.

Day in and day out—and regardless of the noise level on any front—the great bulk of our thought and effort continues to be devoted earnestly to the widespread, quiet, orderly, determined, and little publicized but none the less news-worthy efforts toward developing and advancing an always sounder, more productive, more pleasant, and in all ways a more mutually rewarding association between our managers and their employees.

The range of these efforts is briefly indicated inside.

SALARY ADMINISTRATION
Services Department

All activity here is directed to developing—and promoting the company-wide use of—Salary Administration plans and practices which will inspire salaried personnel to their full usefulness and reward each properly for what he gets done by the application of his own inner resources to the opportunity offered.

Particular attention is given to research and to the development—for decentralized use—of methods for analyzing and evaluating positions, for appraising the performances of holders of those positions, and for keeping abreast of changing conditions to the end that policies and practices are kept up to date as to any altered needs and values.

WAGE ADMINISTRATION
Services Department

Services to field operating components are supplied or available in the areas of wage surveys, wage determination, wage structures, incentive plans, job analysis, wage rate procedures and related wage training and administration practices.

Information about national and local regulations is gathered, condensed, and circulated. National and local wage trends and other developments are kept under observation. Recommendations are made on national and local wage issues.

Most important is the constant research to the end of our ever greater competence in knowing—and doing voluntarily—what's right as to wages by all the proper standards.

EMPLOYEE BENEFITS
Services Department

All activity here is directed to aid the Company to do what's right about benefits and help all concerned obtain full value from the programs.

Every effort is made—through manuals and personal visits—to assist operating components both in the adequate explanation of the benefit plans to employees and in the smooth and economical functioning of the programs in their day to day operation.

Research is constantly pursued as to what's best for the future as well as to what are the current trends and any requirements for improvements to keep our plans comparable and equitable. Related to this research is the frequent cooperation with government groups and other employers in helping with sound benefits legislation.

HEALTH & SAFETY
Services Department

All activity here is directed toward aiding operating components in the development and use of practices which will improve the health of our employees and reduce both the frequency and severity of accidents on and off their General Electric jobs.

Yesterday's accent was on aiding the sick and injured. Today it is on preventing injuries while keeping employees well.

Counsel, training, and appraisal services are provided by our doctors, safety engineers and other responsible key personnel in all areas of health, hygiene, job environment and safety. Advanced research is proceeding in such areas as industrial noise, eye-protection, resuscitation, rehabilitation, and the most effective ways for supervisors to live up to their health and safety responsibilities.

EMPLOYEE COMMUNICATION
Services Department

The aim and effort here is to give aid to operating managers in developing and maintaining effective, two-way communication. This involves both mass and man-to-man techniques.

Help is offered in the development of local communication media and procedures. A special course trains field communication specialists. Company-wide news and other findings are syndicated to employee newspapers and other internal publications. Assistance is given at various locations during periods of local stress. Related research is carried on in the areas of attitudes, motivations, and the oral and written correction of misinformation.

PERSONNEL PRACTICES
Services Department

A consulting service and a wide variety of manuals and other aids are supplied managers to help in the better selection, placement and orientation of supervisory and non-supervisory employees, to help advance employee rating and counselling techniques, to help improve employee upgrading procedures, and to advance sound recreational and other employee services activities.

Workshops on employment practices are held. Courses are given in interviewing and appraising personnel. Training is given in selection tests.

Special research effort is being made again this year on the costly turn-over problem.

EDUCATION & TRAINING
Services Department

This department does research and aids local training directors in their efforts to teach the human side of management. The courses emphasize conference leadership and effective human relations. A series of one-week training institutes is familiarizing local managements with techniques developed and proved to date. Assistance in HOBSO I, HOBSO II, HANEY, and other needed economic education courses continues on a wide and effective scale.

The development course for prospective professional Employee and Plant Community Relations specialists continues. The first ten to complete the comprehensive 27 months course—all college graduates—will be available for regular full-time assignments in the field later this year.

PLANT COMMUNITY RELATIONS
Services Department

This department does research, develops manuals, and otherwise works to aid local management in making itself known to the community as the good employer GE tries to be, known as a fair and productive purchaser of local goods and services, known as a good taxpayer with no bargains asked, known as a good contributor to and worker in all appropriate local causes, and known as a good corporate citizen in the best sense of the word.

This department aids local management also in cooperating with other employers and alerted citizens who are seeking to measure up to the full range of their good citizenship responsibilities, especially as this applies to economic education, moral determination, and political sophistication.

UNION RELATIONS
Services Department

This department conducts the national negotiations with three unions, advises in the negotiation of our 91 other union contracts, and processes the relatively few grievances coming to the national level. It also supplies specialized aid in "crisis" situations. But all this—important and demanding as it is—is only a small part of its over-all work.

The major thought and effort of this department's headquarters staff and regional managers is in research for better solutions to recurring problems and in making available accumulated "know-how." We are seeking, to the fullest extent practicable, a constructive and harmonious relationship with union representatives while satisfying ourselves and an informed union membership that we are doing what's right.

The department's guiding philosophy continues to be: "Labor problems should be thought out—not fought out."

WHAT IT'S ALL ABOUT

All the foregoing is in pursuit of these twin objectives:
(1) Our doing what we should for our employees.
(2) Their doing what they should for us in fair return.

For our part, we are sure that our managers, as never before, are trying to do what's right about pay, benefits, working conditions, information, participation, and the creation of rewarding human associations.

For their part, our employees will just as surely strive to do what's right by our managers through applying interest, skill, care and effort—as they come to know the facts of our fairness and come to feel the warmth of our human interest.

LET THIS BE THE YEAR

We can be certain that 1954 will be full of fresh challenges on all fronts.

But that provides the opportunity for triumphs too.

Let's make this the year of our greatest triumph to date in the growth of our employees' confidence in our competence and determination to do what's right, and in our heart-felt desire to make of our association together a warmly rewarding human experience.

EMPLOYEE & PLANT COMMUNITY RELATIONS
Services Division
New York

15 THE AFTERMATH

The initial relative silence on the union front, which followed the 1948 settlements, did not last long. Our willingness to put everything on the table at once and our thorough and accurate preparations in making up the package seemingly had not only surprised most of union officialdom but also caught them with no ready-made answers simply because they had no experience in a situation of that kind.

But they were soon back on the job in the old way. We regretted—but were not too surprised—that they came back with nothing constructive or new but simply with repetitions of the familiar charges: that we were trying to separate the members from their union officials; that the offer had been made so good because the union officials then could not get the members to strike for more; that both our statement that we did not regard strike threats as convincing and our implication that we would take a strike were unfair tactics; that we were "playing God" in all the talk about the balanced-best-interests; that we could have offered lots more out of our "swollen" profits without having to raise prices; that taking away the forced maintenance of membership was done to weaken unions; that our new program was just a slick device to butter up employees and get a "speed-up" which would yield still more unwarranted profits; that we were in a "capitalist plot against labor's gains"; that we had no business talking over their heads to their members but should communicate only through them; that we knew we would wreck unions if we could ever "get away with" the idea that we were both willing and trying to do right voluntarily.

Before the year was out, there were charges we had made a "secret decision to cancel the contract and try to break up the union." This was followed by "GE takes off its mask" and "GE bares its anti-union fangs." Charges of employees slaving away with "bleeding fingers" and purple passages or hate and defamation were much too common for comfort if you believed anyone was listening and believing—and sad experience dictated that we had better not discount the possibility that the charges were being believed.

At about this time, a union president was reported as pontificating that "when a union becomes respectable, it loses its potency." I for one disagreed completely, but I saw no use in airing my views on that subject when there was so much else that needed saying in employee and community interest.

Surveys and individual contacts with employees clearly showed that few employees still believed that we were engaging in such terrible conduct either at their locations or at our plants elsewhere. This represented a sharp change in employee evaluation of what so many union officials had been saying about us. Also, merchants and other businessmen in our plant cities were beginning not only to appreciate our contributions there but also to understand that we were really trying to earn the favorable regard of others in the communities.

A change in the attitude and conduct of local police and other government politicians was not to be expected until a safe majority of their constituents had first demonstrated convincingly that they had changed theirs. And the union officials—being of necessity under current conditions the politicians they were—also would not change until it had become "good politics" to do so and bad politics to continue on the old destructive course toward our job-supplying and job-improving efforts. Continuing opposition from these quarters was to be expected, but a disturbing fact was that at so many locations the teachers, press, and some influential clergymen—among them the local "intellectuals"—were holding on tenaciously to their outmoded misconceptions about us and even about the private business system in general.

This small sample of such zealous but unwarranted anti-business behavior by some intellectuals may have been misleading. And I may have been even more unjustified in relating this to an impression I had gathered along the way—from reading, from my Washington experience, and from what I had tried to make my much more open-eyed observation since. Nevertheless, it seemed to me that what private business and its five kinds of overlapping beneficiaries were up against—and up against not just from the more-leftist union officials but from a majority of the rest of the public and its thought-leaders (which majority was of course made up almost entirely of the business beneficiaries themselves)—was the result of vast and powerful forces which for a long time had been working covertly through many channels and media. Here is that impression for what it may be worth:

Socialism in any of its various forms had made little progress here—even after the founding of the American Fabian Society in 1895—until Fabian leaders reportedly came over from England in 1898 and succeeded in teaching the few local collectivists how to infiltrate campus faculties with what has been called their "sneaky" brand of British Fabian socialism. This emphasized bringing about socialization here by taking us gradually and voluntarily step-by-step down the same, but unrecognized, path to the very same central socialist dictatorship to which the Communist brand of socialism would have taken us suddenly by violent revolutionary force.

This showed immediate signs of success in a small way in one or two Eastern schools, from which the intellectuals persuaded and trained there went out as "Typhoid Marys" to the rest of the country.

These Fabians seem to have followed here the successful example set abroad of avoiding open use of the socialist tag, adopting the now-familiar "welfare state" and other such semantically pleasing but deceitful trademarks.

Many will disagree, but my own impression is that the so-called New Deal—which came on in 1933 and in which I worked for almost three years in Washington—was nothing "new" at all but only the importation of this 40-year-old Fabian socialism as modified only slightly in the meantime by the theories of Keynes about the wonders of truly massive doses of the spending and deficit dope which has since proved so habit-forming and debilitating here, as in its English home and elsewhere abroad.

But I do not believe that this more attractive and outwardly less frightening Fabian or "welfare state" brand of socialism could ever have generated within itself the money, the manpower, and the competent central directing capacity needed to convert—as we have seen it do—the majority of the public by converting the majority of the public's effective thought-leaders in the schools and colleges, in the press, on the air, in civic and social organizations, and even in too many churches of all major denominations. It could not, by itself, have gained such a determining influence over what is now promised by both parties in campaigns and what the winners do in office. It could not alone have succeeded to the point where—now that we are in the second and even third generation of it—it so largely determines what is taught "at mother's knee."

The needed outside help seemed to come from two vast sources in particular—first from some labor union sources and later from the federal bureaucracy.

Labor unions, like socialism itself, had made little headway here in the nineteenth century. Union organizers must soon have seen the close ideological fit between what the welfare-staters were saying about private business and what they themselves needed to say and have believed about private employers. There was an obvious opportunity for union organizers and these unrecognized socialists to make common cause—no matter whether they worked jointly or went their separate ways—toward their mutually desired ends of discrediting and weakening voluntary private activity, of cutting down free choice and individual responsibility, of attacking private property and limited government, and of building up blind confidence in gang force, central planning, and thinly veiled central dictation.

Most of the union organizers I had observed along the way had seemed to believe it was necessary to utilize the basic socialist party line in order discredit the intentions, practices, and results of private business in both the material and the nonmaterial areas. To do this in the individual plant or company, they apparently judged it necessary or advisable to go beyond the one employer under attack and try to discredit the system itself—that is, discredit the private saving and investment, the free choice in product and job competition, and the principle that rewards must vary in accordance with one's worth to others from whom one wants something in return.

However slowly these forces may have gotten under way around the turn of the century—and whatever relationship they may have maintained during the next 40 years—by the time I reached Washington in World War II there seemed to be a solid antibusiness front maintained largely through the joint or separate activities of (1) the intellectuals from the campuses and other such sources, (2) most of the more vocal union officials and their staffers along with their thousands of local representatives in the field, and (3) the incumbent government officials and their enormously swollen bureaucracy there and throughout the country.

Those then in the ascendancy in Washington were somewhat like bartenders who had taken to drink, for they appeared to have been taken in by their own propaganda that businessmen were crooks and that, while needed for his business experience, a businessman drafted for war work could not be trusted to conduct government affairs with any industry in which he had gained his experience. It is unnecessary to comment on how much dangerous and expensive waste was caused by the sheer impracticability of this mistaken idea.

One relatively unimportant feature of the constant effort to discredit private business, but one which perhaps indicates as vividly as any the antibusiness atmosphere there at the time, was the practice of publishing in the newspapers the pay—mine included—which recent proxies showed those coming to Washington had received in their prior business work, the inference being that no man could honestly earn or properly accept that much.

Another indication of our second-class status in Washington is to be found in a thoughtless breach of etiquette on my part. I was passing through the waiting room just outside the War Production Board chairman's office and spied a high-up business friend cooling his heels with hat in hand. Being absorbed with other things, I waved a simple "hello" and passed on. But down the hall the picture began to register, and I couldn't resist the temptation to bear down from my bureaucratic vantage point and do a little good-natured needling. So I returned, shook hands and, in the hearing of our charming receptionist, said, "It's too bad you are a business official. If you were a union official, you would not have had to wait but would have been ushered right in without even taking off your hat."

But far more important than any of the above was the evidence I felt was all around that the war was being purposely used by many people of top influence to effect a permanent revolution in our society and its government. The enormous war demands were real, and the economic situation was critical, but I suspected there was every intention of having the consequent measures and controls, which were termed "temporary" or "for the duration," continued to a maximum degree in peace time. The extremist socialist revolutionaries of real influence were probably relatively few in number, but their influence was enormous. The responsible members of government seemed to be going along either because they did not realize what was really afoot or because they were reluctant to undertake the corrective economic education of a public already far into the belief that government could spend more than it took. Both the purpose and the trend seemed to be away from freedom and toward authoritarianism, away from individualism and toward collectivism, from willing to unwilling exchange, from a free market to a planned economy, from capitalism to statism, from voluntarism to coercion, from little to big government, from honest dollars to a permanently inflationary course.

And the government was openly using the war emergency as an excuse to give union officials effective help in forcing millions more into the unions and thereby generating the enormous funds which would be used so largely, not only for "educational" work through schools, churches, press, and the air waves, but also for direct and indirect partisan political work in electing favorable government officials. Both kinds of work resulted in furthering the trend noted above and also, to get right down to cases, in increasing the difficulty in 1948 of getting that cooperation which our employees and neighbors should contribute in their own interests.

16 THE SCENE REVISITED

As I review in retrospect the reactions of managers, other employees, communities, and union officials to our efforts from the 1948 settlement on through 1960, I confess to having no different impression of the people and events now than the ones I gathered as we went along. They were these:

1. *Employee Response:* Employees in general, including managers at all levels, believed the Company overall was really trying in the ways claimed, but they were constantly and quite properly sitting in judgment on the degree to which the program seemed to be bearing fruit for them individually through their immediate bosses.

2. *Manager Effectiveness:* There was a distressingly wide variation in the degree of effectiveness of the individual managers at the various levels and locations. This seemed to come from lack of willingness or ability or newly developed habit or all three. Naturally, no matter how hard they tried, some managers just did not have the adaptability and the learning ability for the newly required knowledge and communication skills, and they were falling by the wayside. There was steady improvement, but it seemed distressingly slow at many levels and locations in the face of the recognition and rewarding response the now-expectant employees were proving they would give any improvement. Our greatest continuing effort was to get more rapid improvement in this area.

3. *Union Reaction:* The noisier union officials at the national level, both personally and through their publications, stuck to the old vituperation, palpably wrong information, and outlandishly false charges. This seemed very bad selling, and our truthful product salesmen, for instance, could have hoped for no greater windfall than to have their product competitors act that way.

Such a continued course would also seem likely to be recognized as extremely bad politics by any alert politician. I had felt, on first looking over the field, that union members sooner or later would get the impression that too many of their top and other officials were serving their own interests and objectives rather than those of the members, and some time later there began to appear in the more sober union publications some warnings along these lines from thoughtful and observant officials. What we had hoped for was that—as the members abandoned the false expectations that had been generated and began more unemotionally to examine the realities—the union officials at both national and local levels would settle down to joining in a constructive search for the kind of arrangements which would produce and sustain the most and best jobs. We wanted more help in this than we had been getting, and we had reason to suspect that the members themselves wanted more such help from their union representatives. Meanwhile, the credibility of the misinformation and false charges in the union press had dropped sharply, as our tests demonstrated, and we regretted there had not yet been a constructive replacement.

Union officials at the local level—both as individual observers aware that we were trying to deal with them fairly and in good faith and as politicians more alert than their national officers to membership values and reactions—were showing less patience with the outlandish demands and charges and were demonstrating more interest in getting down to cases to determine what was possible and workable. This increased rather than decreased the support they got from members on the demands that were sensible. And the members obviously wanted to preserve their unions to insure our continued alertness and our being forced up to any proper level we did not appear to want to reach voluntarily, but they were out of patience with efforts to "emote" and rouse them—and get them to lose pay—because of somebody's bad judgment or desire for a silly personal political victory. This did not change the fact that there still was a wide gap—and probably always would be—between what some and what others initially might think was right. Some of these areas of possible mutual misunderstanding and mutual accomplishment will be discussed later.

There were some very regrettable exceptions to this picture of progress with employees and their local union officers, but we could find no case where the continuing difficulties were not due to the local operating managers and their associates individually from top to bottom—and thus collectively—not having carried out the new program properly with both employees and neighbors.

4. *Community Reaction:* Community reaction in the almost 150 plant cities was similar to employee reaction, though less pronounced and slower to improve. Neighbors, too, reflected the feeling that the company overall was trying, but they had less direct contact with the managers than did the employees, and, as already indicated, there was a special problem of resistance on the part of some of the more important local thought-leaders. Also, some of the towns in which we had plants were tougher to convince because of ingrained family hatred of employers dating back before the turn of the century and because, more recently, of prolonged unemployment resulting from most other employers having been driven out of town by unrealistic treatment from unions and local politicians.

But despite a certain hesitancy at some locations in the neighbors really believing what they saw, the communities were in general quite expectant and thus fairly responsive to any visible improvement in our efforts to be both a good and an understood contributor and corporate citizen. All that was required to get our neighbors' help in our usefulness to all was for the local managers to acquire enough of the needed knowledge and skill and then make the appropriate efforts to win the approval and support of neighbors in their own interest.

17 POLITICAL BARGAINING

The union official had always seemed to me to be a politician—as he had to be in my time and as he probably should be any time. He was responsible to his constituency and expendable when his efforts or results were unsatisfactory.

But in the case of this union politician, as well as of a politician in government, the familiar expression, "Oh, he did that for political reasons," usually meant only that he had done something which he knew was wrong for, but sensed would look good to, the misinformed majority of his constituents. In any event, the union politician needed an informed, alert, and sophisticated electorate, or he would have trouble avoiding the temptation to take the easy way of the demagogue in playing upon the current misinformation and wishful thinking of his constituents and even working to build up both of these to produce a much higher level of fancied wrongs and false expectations.

I felt there were two glaring needs in negotiation and other relations with union officials, and neither was the fault or responsibility of the union officials themselves.

One was the lack of a well-enough informed, alerted, and sophisticated membership. A politician cannot be expected to do the corrective work in such a situation. He can add to the pleasant illusions but gets in trouble when taking them away. This kind of job usually must be done by independent thought-leaders in education, religion, press, and elsewhere. Unfortunately, I felt that most of the influences that should have been corrective in my time were, on the contrary, adding to the false expectations. Business-men would naturally be expected to be the last to do this work, since they were theoretically in the poorest position from a credibility standpoint, but what little we in General Electric had tried had been surprisingly well received in the circumstances, considering the odds against us.

The other glaring need was for the employee representative and employer representative to come to the bargaining table more nearly as equals than had been true in the recent past. The trouble with our country's so-called "free collective bargaining" in those days was that it too often turned out to be not free, not collective, and, in fact, too one-sided to be real bargaining at all.

What too often went for bargaining was simply the imposition of a settlement which—no matter how camouflaged—was in the end substantially what the union official had unilaterally decreed or decided, even though for public consumption he might have gone through the motions of cutting his initially too high demands even in half in order to look reasonable.

Any bargaining to be worthy of the name had to involve equals. That is, it had to be between two parties who were relatively equal as to the ability and freedom to accept or reject the other's offer to buy or sell.

The union official, because only his side had been heard, usually arrived at the bargaining table in a position to have his demands automatically considered good and thus to get the unquestioning backing not only of the majority of employees but of the rest of the public and of the public's representatives.

The employer, in contrast, came with practically no such backing and hardly even any credibility in such matters. In fact, what he too often faced was a widespread assumption that, if he wanted or recommended something, it must certainly be bad for employees, bad for consumers, bad for "people," bad for the deserving many, and good only for the greedy, wicked, and undeserving few.

As just one of the many examples of how illogical and unhealth was the imbalance, a union official could feel safe in treating any employer proposal with contempt, whereas if the employer refused to go along with a particular union proposal—or even failed to add further concessions to those already made in the current sessions—he would almost surely be subjected to a "refusal to bargain" charge which would be taken seriously by the NLRB, the press, and too many employees and other members of the public.

We businessmen could not blame this on the union officials or government officials or any other third parties brought into the act, and we only showed how naive we were when we tried to do so. *Any fault was ours entirely, and theirs not at all.* For an unsound settlement was almost sure to be sanctioned by effective public opinion—that is, it had actual public approval, or it would be tolerated by the public, or it was unknown to the public and politicians in unions and government were confident there would be no adverse reaction among the majority if it should become known. In other words, such an unsound settlement was "good politics" with a public that did not realize that it and not the owners would pay the bill.

And we had to face the fact that a substantially lower or different settlement might well have backfired on the union officials involved—that is, it would not have met with favor among employees and neighbors either because of what they already believed or because of what they had been told by the political competitors of the union officials. Of course, this would not have applied if the different and sounder settlement had meanwhile become "good politics," but that was an unlikely development in the highly charged atmosphere of most negotiations and in the very short time available during the formal bargaining period.

Such an improper imbalance of economic and political power, derived from the then-current state of employee and public opinion, could not be corrected by any negotiating expertise after arrival at the bargaining table. It was then too late. For the union official and his dedicated allies—seen and unseen across the community and country—had done their "prior homework" too effectively over the preceding years in the newspapers, in their own and allied publications, and from thousands of public and private platforms; while the employer had neglected his own homework, especially in connection with the controversial issues where the real interest lay and as to which there would have been some chance of being effective. The inevitable result emphasized the old adage that "he who goes in like a lion comes out with the lion's share."

The plain fact seemed to be that the leftist intellectuals, the noisier of the more leftist union officials and their publications and field organizations, and the enormous federal bureaucracy were operating more and more across the country as the ideological detractors of private business and of the concept of free choice, private property, and limited government on which our unique well-being here had been built.

Some union officials seemed to be the central idea suppliers or the idea coordinators or the chief dispensers through their own and the other distributing agencies. They had seemingly become the controlling factor in our country's public opinion formation. The creativeness, efficiency, voluntarism, and essential humanity of the "private sector" were being vilified while the inevitable stultification, wastefulness, and dictatorial regimentation of the "public sector" were being glorified. They were sending or bringing into our plant sites many influences which were causing very damaging employee and community disapproval of and resistance to our objectives, practices, and accomplishments through shameful appeals to prejudice, misinformation, and wishful thinking.

The U.S. Government had seemed to have established to its own satisfaction that there were some few labor union officials of real influence who were Socialists of the "Communist" variety—by which was usually meant that they were in league with Russia against our country. It seemed to me evident that there were many more union officials and staffers—although still few in relation to the total number—who were dyed-in-the-wool Socialist revolutionaries seeking step by step to change fundamentally our free society to a socialist one. My guess, however, was that thousands upon thousands of other union officials at various levels either did not approve of this or were going along not because they were purposeful Socialists but because the attacks were keeping private business managers and owners besmirched, on the defensive, and off balance. Hence the attacks were making organizing and negotiating easy to carry on along the old familiar Socialist Party line of brute, crook, and exploiter and of getting by gang force what was wanted. Such domination of public opinion and of public servants had produced three special and improper privileges which made the already one-sided bargaining all the easier to dominate. They were the following:

The "Anxious Bench"

Management Officials and Union Officials inside at the bargaining table don't have just each other to suit. The real job is to satisfy "The Big Four" waiting anxiously outside. Each of that four has a part to play. But not one of them *can* play it—or will even *try*—unless he thinks he is going to get what's right from the others for what he does.

(Specimen employee-publication article)

1. The designated union's *tight monopoly* of the employer's labor market by reason of the "sole bargaining" provision in both the original Wagner Act and the Taft-Hartley Act. This monopoly was coming to be recognized as the basic source of the union officials' vast economic power and as the basic mistake in the support which the public was continuing to give to union activities. The public was, of course, against monopoly—and especially against such an unregulated one—but had not yet become sufficiently aware that monopoly in this field operated just as much against the public interest as monopoly does anywhere else.

2. The license to impose *compulsory unionism* by means of which unwilling workers are forced, with the cooperation of their employer, to forfeit their jobs unless they give the demanded financial and other support to union officials' ideas and actions regardless of their approval or disapproval. This meant that the unions were no longer the "voluntary associations" they were represented to be, and that union officials had become the masters, instead of the servants or responsive agents, of the members. This automatic flow of money and other support was coming to be recognized as the source of the union officials' excessive political power.

3. The license to engage in *illegal coercion* and even in *illegal violence* to persons and property. This privilege and unlawful immunity was extended to no other citizen or organization. This continued to be tolerated—despite horrendous abuses of people as workers, consumers, and savers—presumably because of an outdated and basically wrong habit of mind which held that "little people" were thus being served and that the cause of the unions was so just that any means was tolerable.

The unwise laws—and the related disgraceful "double standard" of law enforcement—could not be properly corrected until public opinion had been readied for such changes through correction of the misinformation; that is, until it had become "good politics" with effective majorities—nationally and in individual communities—for the changes to be made.

In pointing out the need for such changes during my active association with these problems, I neither suggested nor had in mind anything as silly as discarding or breaking up the unions. I

How Would <u>You</u> Revise Our Labor Laws?

We Americans are about to re-examine—through our Congress—the fundamental laws regulating the relations of employees, unions, and management with each other and the public.

We should be sure this examination is calm and deliberate. Any resulting revisions will be of vital interest to the whole public—to the some 15 million union members and the more than 45 million non-union workers, to union officials and management officials, to consumers and to citizens at large.

Despite any differing points of view, what all of us really seek are laws that are fair to employees, unions, and employers, and which adequately protect the public.

So, let's check the questions on the following pages to see what are some of the individual ingredients you think should or should not be included in any law that would accomplish what we are all seeking.

(First page of four-page ballot on Taft-Hartley Act)

believed they were here to stay, and properly so. As already indicated, I believed they had a perfectly valid reason for existence in the good they could do as compared with the harm that, in my opinion, so many of their unfortunate economic and political activities were doing to their members and the other beneficiaries of business—which, of course, included just about everybody. Any corrections, of course, had to stand up as genuinely in the balanced-best-interests and not be erroneously designed to serve any special interest.

The following policy assurance—sent to all employees over the company's and my signatures on April 2, 1948, just as we were getting well into that first year's negotiations with the 20 unions—was sincerely meant and had no reason to be revised in my remaining 13 years there. Here it is in full with no word changed except for the elimination of two paragraphs about a wage situation applicable only to that year.

HOW DOES GENERAL ELECTRIC FEEL ABOUT UNIONS?

This is the time of the year when our relations with unions representing our employees come in for the greatest general attention and scrutiny. We are having annual meetings with one after another of the 20 unions that now represent various groups of our employees. Negotiations have already been in progress sometime with a few of these, including the union that represents the largest number of bargaining units.

That is why we feel that right now our employees and their neighbors may have more than usual concern about the attitude of the company towards unions, the leadership of them, and membership in them.

Here's How We Feel About It

General Electric accepts the idea of free labor unions as thoroughly in keeping with the basic freedoms guaranteed to all individuals and institutions by our Constitution and our way of life.

We believe that these basic freedoms—possessed by us all here—offer a special opportunity for business and labor organizations to work together for the good of customers, employees, stockholders, and the public in a way that will benefit each without penalizing any.

We believe firmly and sincerely in the right of our employees to join a union, if they want to, and to join the union of their choice.

Likewise, we believe equally in the right of our employees not to join a union, if they do not want to, and not to remain union members if they don't want to.

We believe that the presence or absence of unions at General Electric should depend solely on the wishes of our employees. We believe joining or not joining a union should be the choice solely of the individual employee.

We believe that neither the company nor labor organizations should attempt through any coercion to influence the decision by our employees on the question of whether or not there should be a union or the question of whether or not the individual employee should join.

What About Union Leadership?

General Electric recognizes the complete right of union members to exercise their own free choice in the election of officers. We believe the members in free elections will select those officers they believe will represent the best interests of the membership in both short-term and long-range problems.

This does not mean that we claim all union officers so elected will be good, any more than we would claim all business men are good. We would not be believed or respected if we did make any such claim.

But whether we believe these leaders are good or bad, we will go right along dealing in good faith with them as long as they are accredited to us as the regularly elected officers of any union certified by the National Labor Relations Board as a bargaining agent.

Whether or not a union leader agrees with us or is easy to deal with does not make him good or bad in our estimation. The good union leader—for what our impression may be worth—is the one who acts as the servant of the members and who wisely and sincerely represents the short-term and long-range best interests of the people he is supposed to represent.

Incidentally, we think that what is best for both the short-term and long-range interests of employees will be almost exactly what is also best for the short-term and long-range interests of customers, stockholders, management, and general public.

In the matter of going along with union leaders' aims and claims, we believe the policy of our employees and the policy of our company should be one and the same in principle. We believe both employees and management should support and cooperate with union officers in any proposal that is sound. We believe both employees and management should feel equally free to withhold support and cooperation where any particular proposal of union representatives is honestly believed to be unsound.

What Does The Record Show?

General Electric was a good place to work before there were unions of any consequence. General Electric has continued over the years to become steadily a better and better place to work—and, in most places where there have been unions, they undoubtedly have been responsible for some aid to management's accomplishments along this line.

THE GOOD WAY

Good Progress

High wages–Low prices?

We can have them!

LET'S LEARN FROM BRITAIN

FOUR YEARS AGO the British working man voted himself relief from the trials and tribulations of capitalism.

Laws were passed guaranteeing prosperity and security to the workers.

The only catch was that prosperity does not come from passing laws: It comes from producing more goods and services.

What Is a Speed-Up?

And what is just an honest day's work?

(Specimen headlines from articles in employee publications)

Over the years General Electric has made continuous effort to iron out the differences of opinion or interest between employees and the company, and many of the issues have been settled or reduced substantially. As a result, the areas of constructive agreement are tremendous, although the headlines would sometimes lead people to believe otherwise. But we believe some disagreement is healthy and productive, as it stimulates further accomplishment and further knowledge of the opportunities and limitations that surround our joint activities.

How Do Matters Stand Now?

*   *   *

If General Electric were hostile towards unions certified to it as bargaining agents by the National Labor Relations Board, the company could have recently cancelled certain contracts and thus forced several unions into embarrassing difficulties and considerable expense. This the company chose not to do, and in these several cases is going along with the existing contracts as previously negotiated except for such changes as may have been made necessary by law or as may be found mutually agreeable.

We will continue to try to cooperate in every proper way with our employees directly or with unions that are certified as the representatives of their choice.

GENERAL ELECTRIC COMPANY

18 BARGAINING EXAGGERATIONS

The union official, to be a sufficiently intelligent and adequately responsible representative, would have to try his capable best to see that his members got not only no less, but also no more, than their fair share in the five-way contributor-claimant arrangement that would take all along together toward accomplishing the values which would yield the most and the steadiest jobs at the pay that was appropriate in all the circumstances.

1. *The Skin of the Gnat:* As already noted, the untruthful and otherwise short-sighted employer—who made no offer, then 2½ cents, then the full five cents he had known all the time was what he should and would eventually offer—lost the confidence of his employees and neighbors not only in this but in other even more important matters, as was of course intended by the union and richly deserved by the employer.

Seemingly blind that this kind of inevitable consequence could be expected by him also, the union official would characteristically work all year at trying to stir up emotional employee and community support for a string of obviously unrealistic demands totaling as much as twice what both the employees and neighbors suspected he really wanted and intended to get in the coming bargaining. Despite the growing disenchantment with this and the resulting loss of credibility in other areas, too many union officials kept up this practice apparently through sheer habit and lack of alertness or because they still believed they would look good or reasonable when appearing to compromise to a lower figure; or because they hoped the lower settlement would make the employees mad and thus give stronger support at the next bargaining; or to make it seem there was "a wide difference between the parties" which would justify the intercession of government or other outside mediators or arbiters.

117

Another unfortunate result of this deceptive kind of bargaining was the belief of many union officials that, no matter how intrinsically good it was, an initial or subsequent offer just was not acceptable unless it had been either offered or revised in a way that would serve the political needs of the union officials. In other words, the final settlement had to appear not only to have been forced out of us but also to contain a forced extra ingredient which represented a politically adequate amount more than we had shown we believed was right and were willing to grant. Time and again I was told in private—and even occasionally before mediators and 20 or 30 others at the bargaining table—that there was nothing wrong with the offer except that it was ours and not theirs, and that they had to justify themselves with their members by showing they could force something more of importance out of us. To indicate the absurd dimensions which this could occasionally reach, a negotiator was once urging—before three mediators, a lady, and 15 or 20 others—that I add "just some little something" extra which would "hardly cost a thing" but which could be blown up to look pretty good and thus serve his need. My recollection of what he then added—necessarily cleaned up a little now for publication even though a lady was present at the time—was substantially this: "You don't seem to understand that I can stretch the skin of a gnat over a couple of box cars."

In response to the continual appeals to "cooperate" with them in meeting their political needs—by which could only be meant our willingly helping them fool our employees and neighbors about us as well as about the union officials themselves—we kept replying that we did not think either they or we could get away with such stuff any longer; that, for ourselves, we did not want to and would feel silly to try; and that, if they wanted to go on trying in this area, a much more promising possibility for credibility might lie in claims that they had persuaded or forced us to make the good offers in the first place together with any later improvements. But the only visible effect of this advice in my time was a statement after one offer to the effect that "We have forced this out of them. Now let's force some more."

Obviously, such union officials could be diverted from so futile and wasteful a course only by still firmer conviction on the part of employees and community—reflected in still firmer insistence to the union officials involved—that the union officials should sensibly work at genuinely constructive activities in employee and community interest.

2. *Confusion about "Productivity":* It was hard to tell in the beginning whether some union officials were themselves confused about productivity or were relying on the ignorance of their members. But the outlandish claims which were made publicly about what members were due on the basis of productivity gains—even after we had been over the ground repeatedly with both the members and the union officials—seemed ample evidence that the officials knew better but believed their members still did not.

As just one typical example of the wild claims that were made, one union in 1954 came up with a pretended discovery that over the preceding five years our production had doubled, and our productivity per worker had gone up 50 percent. This was nonsense of the most amateurish sort.

What had really happened was this: Our total billings in dollars had almost doubled from 1949 to 1953. Factors contributing to this were (1) a net increase of 52,000, or 30 percent, in the number of employees, (2) a sharp increase in overtime, (3) a change in the product mix and in the ratio of the work done inside to the amount of outside purchases and subcontracting, and (4) a price rise of 17 percent as a necessary result of the new steep Korean war taxes and the otherwise inflated material and labor costs. Our wage rates had gone up about 28 percent, as against a 13-percent rise in the cost of living.

Not only did the productivity per employee plus his machines not increase by the claimed 50 percent, but there was no evidence that our employees, good as we felt they were trying to be, had been able to increase their average accomplishment at all by means of their own inner resources of skill, care and effort. Just the opposite had almost surely happened despite their best efforts to achieve a good rate of production with a minimum of spoilage and other waste. For, to get a net increase of 52,000 in our employment—as we had over the preceding five years in the face of the draft and a sellers' market on labor—we had had to recruit and train over 175,000 new employees and to upgrade many thousands not ready for more skilled or responsible work.

A point to be especially noted here is the fact that the interrelationship of wage increases, price increases, and cost-of-living increase will vary widely from company to company depending on the current opportunity to mechanize. General Electric's 28-percent rise in wages and 17-percent rise in prices—as against a 13-percent rise in cost of living—meant that General Electric and its thousands of competitors in the various lines on a weighted average basis had not been able to mechanize, or otherwise make savings to offset pay and material price increases, as fast as had the average of all businesses whose products are reflected in the cost-of-living index. I do not have the figures now, but it is safe to guess that the automobile industry had done better than the average, as had General Electric's lamps, appliances, and small motors, whereas our heavier and more "custom-built" products made in small numbers were probably on the low side. It is also probable that manufacturing businesses mechanized and made offsetting savings about twice as fast as service industries.

Wage increases comparable to our 28 percent must have been spread fairly uniformly across the country—or uniformly enough for this illustration—and simply added their part to the inflationary process through the procedure already described. They resulted not in prices being raised that exact amount in each competing industry but in prices being about that much higher than they would have been, after the effect of the industry's technological and other advances, had there been no wage increases. The widely varying technological and competitive advances were not, and could not have been, diffused through the wage structure; they were, and had to be, diffused to the public through the widely varying contributions, industry by industry, via the price structure.

An industry which, with other factors constant, had a 5-percent wage increase, a 5-percent productivity increase, and no price increase was inflationary to the same extent that an industry would be with a 5-percent wage increase, no productivity increase, and the consequently required price increase. Incidentally, this again demonstrated our country's good fortune in being able to supply a market for so many desirable products which had been made in the great volume that permitted the mechanized mass production in the first place and which lent themselves to progressively more mechanization as it became necessary to offset the artificially high pay and thus maintain the ability to offer attractive values.

Some of the union officials continued to show actual or pretended confusion between output divided by the number of employees, that is, output per employee and his machines on the one hand and output per employee from his own inner resources on the other. It was the worth of the latter, of course, that was the proper measure of employee pay. And we continued to supply managers, all other employees, and the union officials with explanatory material aimed at being helpful toward a realistic sense of values with respect to productivity. Just one example is the following message sent to all employees on August 10, 1951—reproduced here in full with no word changed:

TWO KINDS OF WORK
... AND PAY

The important work of the world is made up of what men do and what machines do.

Men

The American worker doesn't use just his muscles. He works with his mind too. And he gets paid at the *going rate* for the value of the combination of skill, care, and effort *he puts into* the particular kind of work he does.

He cannot in fairness be penalized for poor selling, reckless finance, unwise risks, lack of research, inadequate equipment, poor judgment as to what product to make, or even plain bad luck on the part of management. Likewise, he cannot in fairness lay claim to any of the profits that arise from the better handling of these matters by one management as compared with another.

He does not think it fair for him to be subjected to the uncertainties or the ups and downs of profits and losses occurring because of acts or forces beyond his control. He insists he be paid the going rate for what *he puts into* the work—regardless of whether his employer is unable to make both ends meet or is making a little or a lot of profit as compared with the fellow across the street or in the next town—and *he is right.*

Machines

The machine does a different kind of work, and that work gets paid for—if at all—on a different basis.

Power plants, factories, tools, designs, and advanced methods not only take most of the *hard work* out of work, but also multiply a given amount of human attention and energy into a vastly expanded output over what would be possible by hand work alone. The machine a man runs may use 100 or 1,000 times the power he himself could exert.

Where an individual actually causes some of this increase in output—through the skill, care, and effort *he puts into* the work at his particular job rather than through the extra work the new machine does—he is rewarded accordingly in his day-to-day pay, whether others of his fellow employees are making similar advances or not and whether the business is or is not making a profit.

But that steady rise in output per worker—which we have come to expect will more than offset the sharp decline in physical effort and hours of work—is due almost entirely to the constant application of the new equipment and technology provided by management with share-holders' money.

These mechanical multipliers of human effort are provided out of the savings of people who deny themselves the products and services their money could buy at any given time; and who take the risk of getting a future reward in the form of profit. They make it possible for the American worker to produce—and buy with his pay—the extra things like the food, clothing, housing, autos, radios, inside plumbing, movies, and a thousand other items which make him the envy of the rest of the world.

But those who have risked their savings do not get 100 or 1,000 times what the worker gets. They get much *less* than the worker. Their "pay" is not only small in comparison, but is irregular and even uncertain. For they have taken the risk of getting only what, *if anything,* is left after all others have been paid for their goods and services. They do not get any specific going rate or any "cost-of-living" adjustments. Their pay may—and frequently does—go down while the pay of the worker is going up.

At General Electric

After we had taken care of all our more than $693 million of outside expenses and taxes for the first half of this year, General Electric had about $490 million left to pay for the two kinds of work.

It took about 86% of that—or $420 million—to pay the new high going rate to our more than 200,000 employees for the skill, care, and effort they put into their work. This was *more* in total—and *more* per employee—than in the first half of last year.

The remainder of that $490 million—or about $70 million (equal to 5.9 cents per dollar of sales)—belonged to our more than 250,000 shareholders for the use and risk of their savings in supplying arm-lengthening equipment and methods. This was *less* than was left for the shareholders in the first half of last year. It was also just about one-sixth of what was paid to our employees—and yet was for getting a heavy and important part of the work done.

And, of course, the shareholders didn't actually get even the 5.9 cents earned per dollar of sale. For, as usual, they put a good part of their earnings—2.3 cents per dollar of sale this time—back into the business for the strength and growth which mean greater future security and opportunity for General Electric employees.

GENERAL ELECTRIC COMPANY

Reproduced below is another example of our continuing efforts to help all concerned keep vividly in mind the relationship between the pay for the one kind of work and the pay for the other. This was distributed on April 23, 1954.

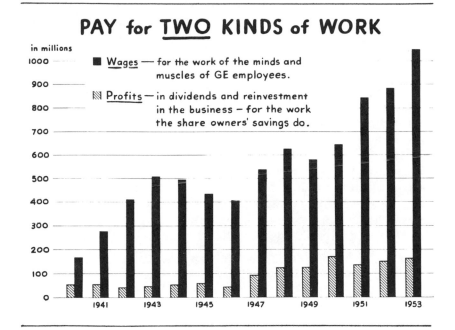

PAY for TWO KINDS of WORK

3. *So-called "Ability to Pay"*: The prenegotiation build-ups in the press and in poorly attended union meetings—as well as in the early negotiation sessions—put unusually heavy emphasis on General Electric's past and current profits as a principal reason why all the relevant and irrelevant economic demands should be granted. This was the old "ability to pay" argument, advanced so many times before in dealing first with the largest or most

profitable company in an industry, and then just as often discarded by the union itself as spurious and unworkable.

This "ability to pay" argument was exactly contrary to what I felt was the valid basic union contention that employees doing the same work under the same circumstances should get the same pay. If "ability to pay" should become the yardstick for measuring pay, then those employees working for companies making high profits would get higher pay than those working for companies making low profits, and those working for companies operating at a loss would have to suffer pay cuts. The workers would not stand for any such thing—and no union would dare make such arrangements—except in an isolated and unusual circumstance of trying temporarily to save jobs with an employer about to fold up.

Of course, to judge from experience as well as the obvious, the union officials had no intention of letting ability to pay be the measurement. Yet union officials—who were high in the counsels of Presidents of the United States, who were approved by professors at leading graduate schools of business administration, who had effective support from many prominent clergymen in the various faiths, and who enjoyed a most favorable press—would openly and inexplicably and unashamedly take the chance of going through this one-two procedure: First, try to settle with the most profitable producer on the basis of his so-called "ability to pay." Next, to shift promptly 180 degrees from ability to pay and demand the same amount from all other employers on the basis that a firm "pattern" had been set for them to follow regardless of their ability—or inability—to pay.

In our own negotiations, this demand was never taken very seriously by either side and never seemed to be a real issue at the bargaining table itself. But the union and allied sources of propaganda against the competitive profit system kept up the demand in the union and public press, presumably as an additional possible means of engendering further emotional antipathy toward so-called "big business." In any event, we thought it necessary to make periodic statements which we hoped would help all concerned keep their facts straight and increase their sophistication.

The example given below was the first of our efforts on this subject. The second paragraph has been modified from the original, but only to the extent, out of politeness, of removing the names of some high government officials. Otherwise, it is exactly as sent to all our managers, our other employees, and our union officials on December 19, 1947.

SHOULD WAGES GO UP–
AND DOWN–WITH PROFITS?

Has this been tried?   Did it work?

Would it be fair to you–if it could work?

The idea that wages in a given company should go up–and down–with the company's profits has been re-born many times. It has had to be discarded just as often. With each rebirth it gets a new name in the hope that its previous failure will be forgotten.

As recently as the winter of 1945-46 this old theory was brought out with another brand new and attractive name–"ability to pay." U.S. Department of Commerce economists and other experts claimed that some companies could raise wages 25% and still make a profit next year–without raising prices. Then the Presidential "Fact Finding" Board got the needed backing in its estimate of 18½ cents as what the biggest steel company and the biggest automobile manufacturer could afford to pay out of the next year's profits.

And what happened this time?

Sober judgment bowed to pressure–
and a "national pattern" was born

The steel maker and the automobile maker had to meet this 18½ cent wage demand because of the public pressure which followed such high blessing from Washington. They reluctantly gave in after strikes despite their expressed conviction that prices would certainly have to go up–which they rapidly did.

The action of these two single companies actually resulted in setting a new national pattern of wage increases–a new level of wages for the entire country. Why? because employees and labor leaders quite naturally demanded immediately, and soon got, similar increases from companies in hundreds of cities and towns all over the United States.

After the first important company in a community gave a raise, then all the other employers there also had to do practically the same–regardless of whether they were making a profit or operating at a loss.

1947 repeated the "national pattern" act

By the spring of 1947 the machinery for suddenly creating a "national pattern" was so well oiled that action by just three or four companies in one industry, under attack for their seemingly large profits, was sufficient to set off a round of similar increases all over the country. As a result, employers in every community were again forced to give practically the same wage increases, no matter whether they were operating at a profit or at a loss. It was demonstrated all over again that a raise in the wage level of most any one of several leading companies could widely influence basic community wage rates in practically every city and town in the United States. A wage raise by any leading company inevitably sets a new value locally on the skill, care, and effort for each particular job there.

High prices washed out the wage "gains"

In the cases of both the 1946 and 1947 flat wage increases, the immediate result of everybody having more pay was more inflation—more take-home money but no more take-home from the grocery. The pleasant illusion of big pay in dollars was short-lived, as rising prices soon cancelled out almost completely what had been misrepresented to the worker as his "gain" in pay. As is usual when everybody gets a pay increase at once—with no more production—then everybody has to hand over the bigger income for the same old production. The buying power of money has simply been cheapened.

More wages—but no more goods

In both cases the 60 million people in the nation's work force got extra dollars for the same old production. But when they turned around to buy each other's production for use by themselves, they found they had to pay all those same extra dollars. Too often they had to pay even more than their extra dollars, because all the arguments about these increases and the accompanying work stoppages cut production and raised costs further. Also, too many workers were fooled into thinking they now had bigger real incomes and could stay away from work and be less careful about spending—thus further forcing up costs and bidding up prices.

Personal performance should set pay

Two companies in the same community may not have the same ability to meet these higher wage costs. One may be making a good profit. The other may be just keeping its head above water. But to hold its employees, the less able company must meet the new community rate set by the other company.

The same situation might arise in a large company between its own plants in different cities, or between its two plants in the same town, or between two different departments in the same plant. One plant or department might be selling its product at a profit due to efficiency or due even to forces beyond its control. The other plant or department might be operating at a loss due to poor efficiency or to bad luck. Quite obviously, the employees at each location should be paid what is right in the circumstances for what they accomplish within the area under their control. They should not be rewarded or penalized for conditions beyond their control.

It would be very unfair for two neighbors to get different pay in the same town for the same work under the same conditions—just because the management where one worked was able or lucky enough to make a good profit while the other management was barely breaking even.

The worker wants to be paid what is right in that community—all things considered—for the skill, care, and effort he puts forth. He can only be held responsible for things under his control, and he wants to be paid for what he accomplishes in this area under his control.

He cannot in fairness be penalized for poor selling, reckless finance, poor judgment as to what product to make, unwise risks, lack of research, or even plain bad luck on the part of management. Likewise, he cannot in fairness lay claim to any of the profits that arise from the sounder handling of these matters by one management as compared with another.

He does not think it desirable or fair for him to be subjected to the uncertainties or the ups and downs of profits and losses occurring because of acts or forces beyond the area under his control.

The worker insists he be paid the going community rate for what he accomplishes in the area under his control, and he is right. Why? Because that's the only basis that would be fair to him.

General Electric Company

4. *Compulsory Unionism:* After eliminating maintenance of membership by agreement in 1948, we were thereafter besought at almost every national negotiation to grant the so-called "union shop." For any who may not already understand this technical and often misleading term, "union shop" did not just mean a shop where there was a union; on the contrary, it meant a shop where an employee was forced, under penalty of loss of livelihood, to join and support a union even if he did not feel the need of any union at all, or did not approve of the particular union or of its officers' actions or what they were doing with his money, or just disagreed in principle with his personal freedom being thus invaded.

The virtues of the union shop, according to the union negotiators, were that it would be in the American tradition of majority rule; would produce a stronger union and make all pay alike for what the union did; would free the officials from having to persuade employees to join and thus give them more time and money to spend on more fruitful activities; and would make the officials more likely to cooperate with the management than if the

THE FREEDOM WE FIGHT FOR

FREEDOM!

Freedom is something we have to *work* for *all* the time — and fight for *most* of the time.

What is this freedom we work and fight for? And — if we get it and keep it — what's it worth?

Let's look.

In 1951 — as in 1776, 1812, 1861, 1917 and 1941; in foreign lands and in our own land — we are fighting *against* tyranny, and *for* the freedom of all nations and all people to live in peace and independence.

We are fighting *against* hatred, fear, greed, intolerance.

We are fighting *for* freedom of speech . . . freedom of religion . . . freedom of assembly . . . freedom from unreasonable searches and seizures . . . freedom from cruel and unusual punishments.

The rights we fight for are the rights of free men . . . the right to trial by jury . . . the right *not* to be deprived of life, liberty or property without due process of law . . . the right to work when and where we please or *not* to work . . . the right to bargain and trade freely

This kind of freedom is not some vague and far-off idea just to be read about, or for children just to

sing about, or for orators just to make speeches about.

This kind of freedom is real. It is the most important thing in our whole lives.

Such freedom *can* be taken away from us by a brutal foreign aggressor, of course. But it can also be taken away from us *by ourselves* — through slipping into the easy habit of turning over to government each new problem, along with an equal amount of individual freedom each time.

Let's rout out this dangerous thief to our freedom that lies hidden in ourselves. Let's put him in chains . . . first by learning the facts of how we can go on living and working together — to the greater benefit of all. And then, by the payment of proper taxes and use of proper restraint and sacrifices in our daily lives — all of which will prevent further inflation. And finally by continuing now as we have in the past to produce, to save, to invent, to improve, to take risks — and to reward each other in accordance with the contribution each of us makes as a free man.

If a man is not free, he is not a *man*. Let's be men enough to work and fight for our freedom — so that we can continue to be men.

(Excerpts from article in employee publication)

latter continued what they claimed was its obviously anti-union opposition to the union shop.

In contrast, I had personally long felt there was ample evidence that compulsory union membership was wrong in principle and bad in practice; that it had proved in practice that it violated the individual worker's freedom of choice, fostered the growth of union monopoly which to me was as vicious as any other kind of monopoly, and opened unions to possible control by racketeers and protected demagogues; that such absolute power to "tax" a worker and make him pay the tax or lose his job gave the union officials an unearned and dangerous power not only over employees and management but also, as was becoming more and more visible, over the rest of the public and its government.

Union officials were themselves among the most zealously vocal in attacking the evils of monopoly in the hands of others. In their own hands, however, they claimed it was an instrument of the highest economic and social virtue and usefulness. But since only one side was talking, this obvious contradiction was going largely unchallenged.

It seemed to me that the term "union security," as applied to the union shop, was a euphemism of the first order, and that the union officials' keen desire for the union shop meant they were seeking security for themselves against the employees rather than security for the employees against somebody else. I naturally hoped I was wrong about this, but I honestly could not find much evidence that I was.

It also seemed to me that the so-called "free rider" consequences were exactly opposite to those claimed by the advocates of compulsory unionism. These claims were, of course, that those who presumably benefited from the union officials' activities should help pay the union expenses and that, where they did not join, they were not only getting free what the members paid for but also were putting the members to extra expense for what they did get.

I believed there was compelling evidence in union experience itself which completely refuted these claims—evidence that confirmed what had been learned throughout history about the gaining and losing of freedom. For the vast majority of union members certainly wanted their union officials to be realistic and nondestructive in their demands, sensible in their pay-endangering adventures, economical in their administration, and devoted to serving the long- and short-term interests of the members.

But even in a case where 100 percent of the employees were voluntary union members, they still could not be sure their union officials would always be responsive servants rather than arbitrary masters, unless the officials—as well as their successors of unknown bent—were subject to one or both of these restraints:

1. The freedom of the individual employee to join or not join the union, and to withdraw after joining if he did not like what was going on.

2. The politically convincing example of a small or large number of employees who had successfully persisted, for reasons they obviously thought to be compelling, in refusing to succumb to the usually terrific pressures to join.

According to this view, the so-called "free rider" did indeed make an economic contribution to the members. Far from inflating members' expenses, he actually kept them down. And he provided other valuable safeguards. As Supreme Court Justice Louis D. Brandeis put it:

> "A nucleus of unorganized labor will check oppression by the union as the union checks oppression by the employer."

Possibly because of our firm stand and our obvious willingness to be forthright in our employee and public communications on the subject, this demand was never really "put to the touch" at the bargaining table in any serious way and I do not recall its ever being admitted as the real reason for any strike threat or strike action—although we and apparently some government officials involved suspected that a strike at one important plant had in reality been called solely to get the union shop even when this was denied by union spokesmen.

However, the "union shop" or "union security" issue continued to be plugged in sections of the union press and by allies in other areas, and we felt it advisable to keep our employees advised as to why we did not believe the union shop would be good for them and why we did not want to be the determining factor in forcing unwilling employees to join, pay dues, and otherwise support a union against their wishes or better judgment. An example of one such communication, which went to all employees on August 17, 1951, is here quoted in full with no word changed:

FREEDOM OR FORCE

We have made it very clear in the past that we are *for* whatever protects the freedom, dignity, and self-respect of our employees.

We are *for* the individual employee being free to choose whether or not he joins a union—and whether, once in, he stays in or gets out. We are *for* his having the opportunity every so often—if he wants it—to choose a new union, or to confirm his previous choice of an old one, or to decide to have none at all.

This is all a matter between the union and the employee. But, we are against his being *forced* to belong to a union, and pay dues, in order to hold a job with us. We don't want to have to sign any contract protecting the union against an employee's freedom of choice.

We want to provide the individual job and to offer the pay, working conditions, and other benefits that are right for that job in each case. In return, we simply ask that the individual employee apply his full skill, care and effort to that particular job—whether he deals with us directly or through a union.

* * * * *

Discussions of these principles of ours come up pretty regularly around the calendar in our periodic negotiations with various of our half a hundred unions. Frequently the demand is renewed for "union security" in the form of the so-called "union shop."

"Union security" is the term for some provision in a contract by which the employer gives the union officers some security against employees. The so-called "union shop" is not just a place where there is a union. It really means that all employees must join a given union and pay dues to that union or lose their jobs.

To just two out of the many unions with which we deal, the union shop would force our employees to pay dues of more than $2.5 million per year. At present, dues at only a little over half of that rate are being checked off for these two unions.

* * * * *

We think it would be wrong for the Company to agree with union leaders that all *present* employees must join a particular union and pay dues or lose their jobs. We think it even more wrong for management to agree that all *future* employees must be "frozen" by the decision of a current majority of *present* employees—and so lose their freedom, as individuals, to decide for or against paying dues to a given union without losing their jobs.

The union shop is most undemocratic—despite claims to the contrary. This becomes clear if we apply "union shop" ideas to local politics. We would be shocked, for example, if a state should go Republican, and all present Democrats and all future citizens of the state should have to join the Republican Party and contribute money to its support or else be compelled to lose their citizenship and jobs and leave the state.

Union security seems to be worth a great deal to union officials. To get the union shop—for their own "security"—union officials often intimate that management will be compensated through being freed from so many strikes, so many grievances, and so many intemperate demands now encountered because the employees are not bound under the discipline of the "union shop." The idea is, of course, that, without losing their jobs the employees can't quit the union and stop paying dues—even when they think the union leaders are doing as they please instead of properly promoting the interest of the employees.

* * * * *

Union leaders condemn employees who stay out of the union as "free riders." We agree that good union leaders should and will merit the *voluntary* support of the members. We believe that good unions can eventually become the "voluntary associations" they are in law supposed to be.

But—in the absence of leaders running the unions in a way that would win voluntary support—we don't think that the Company, as a third party, should discharge employees who don't pay dues.

Absolute power corrupts men and institutions because it prohibits constructive criticism, minority rights, outspoken opposition. Dictatorial power, such as the union shop gives to union officials, makes the union the master rather than the servant of the employees.

This absolute power to "tax" an employee and make him pay the tax or lose his job—is proved by history to give union officials power that is almost immediately abused. For instance, they tend not to give so much of their time to the bread-and-butter matter of wages, hours and working conditions with the particular employer, but to enter the political arena and use their union funds and organizational facilities in ways that have often been notorious despite attempts to curb such activities by law. As a consequence, the unwilling dues contributor has often found himself indirectly financing activities which may be contrary to his more firmly held beliefs.

An individual employee should be free to make the decision as to whether or not he will pay towards the national or international political activities of a union. An individual employee should be free to decide whether his funds will be used by a union as economic power against sound public finance, or against sound improvements in equipment and methods, and so hold back what could otherwise be a rise in the standard of living through workers having their day's work and pay provide more goods per person to enjoy.

*   *   *   *   *

At this time a series of new representation elections at our plants is being sought by many unions. Some of the elections so far this year—and many of the very important ones last year—have varied in their results from a fairly wide to a very narrow majority for the particular union or non-union choice.

But, under our present platform of employee freedom, any large or small number of our employees is, in each case, still left free to belong to the union in power, or to stay out of unions entirely, or to support solely that union which they hope may be successful in gaining the representation rights at some later date.

The whole basis of our republic is that here in America we will protect the minority against unrestricted majority rule . . . and especially against *any* tyranny by the majority.

GENERAL ELECTRIC COMPANY

5. *Thunders of Silence:* It seemed to me there was no area where we well-intentioned businessmen in and out of General Electric had been acting as unnaturally—both as managers and as upstanding private citizens—as in meeting thunders of undeserved condemnation with thunders of silence.

As was customary at the time of the 1948 negotiations, we had agreements not to publicize what was going on until a settlement had been reached. This was an arrangement and a habit I strongly believed should be broken in the interests of employees and others—including even the responsible local union officials. Rumors would fly around the shops and communities raising false expectations and false fears alike and putting responsible people in the management and unions at the mercy of the most irresponsible person around. All this resulted in needless loss of production and needless worry on the part of too many good people.

Another disadvantage to this was that the more vocal unions did a job on us all year in their own and other publications—we

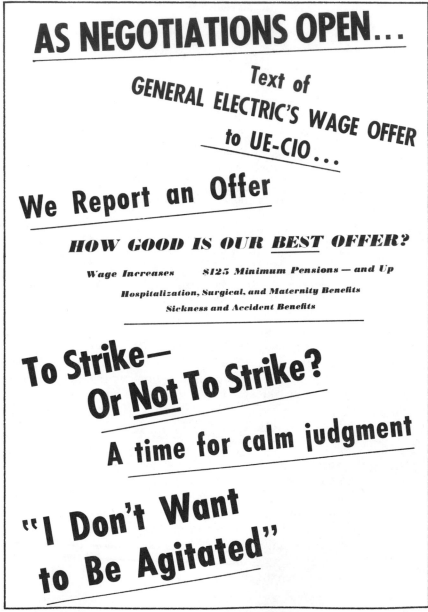

(Specimen headlines from articles in employee publications)

called it "bargaining in the newspapers"—and, when they arrived at the bargaining table, their case was all in. Obviously it was to their tactical advantage to keep us quiet.

We succeeded in getting agreement, however reluctant, on lifting the ban. Thereafter we tried to teletype reports of discussions or developments to the plants and offices once or twice a day during the negotiations, and these were reproduced for distribution to employees, union stewards, local press, and anyone else who was interested. We tried to make these reports factual, and assured the unions we would make public admission and correction of any error instantly upon becoming aware of one. The teletype proved so helpful in substituting fact for emotion that we later set up our own network independent of the regular company system.

We also began summarizing the week's developments on the negotiations front—as well as the other items we were carrying—in the *Employee Relations News Letter* to management, which, as already noted, normally went out every Friday night and was on 15,000 desks internally every Monday morning. We sent the letter to all union officials who asked for it. Here too we tried to make sure that the facts were accurate and the opinions made sense. These bulletins were received with growing confidence and relief by the managers—and apparently elsewhere, as this incident indicates: I had dropped into one of the bargaining sessions of our chief negotiator, Mr. George Pfeif, and was about to reach for a chair, when a very capable and sensible member of the union bargaining committee jumped up and, ignoring the proceedings, poked his finger at me and said, "Hey, I saw a foreman showing that letter of yours to one of our members." Asked what the foreman's name was, he replied, "Nothing doing—you would promote him." Assuring him I had nothing whatever to do with promoting foremen—as he well knew anyway—I then asked him what was wrong with the letter, reminding him of our oft-repeated offer to admit and correct publicly any untruth or other mistake. Thereupon, with a broad grin, he said, "Aw, that's what's wrong. Our people know that you have to tell the truth and that we don't. It's unfair."

(Specimen headlines from articles in employee publications)

Both truth and Mr. Pfeif were involved in another incident which occurred during a session with a very stout and tough bargaining committee. A brand-new member of this committee broke in on something Mr. Pfeif was saying and hotly stated, "That's not so!" Whereupon the long-time head of the union committee fixed the newcomer with a look that would kill, and sternly said: "Listen! If Mr. Pfeif says it's so, it's so!"

As the local managers were freed to talk with the press—and as they grew in skill at appreciating what information was needed or wanted—they became steadily better news-makers in their own right. This was most helpful, especially in view of the awful stuff that continued to come into the local papers from outside.

The increasingly wide gap between the truth as to what was going on in our plants and in actual union relations on the one hand, and what the national press and wire services were prone to carry in considerable volume on the other, was not just disquieting but serious. The news media seemed willing to run the most senseless charges or other cock-and-bull stories at face value; sometimes they could not reach us for comment, and sometimes they failed even to try, assuming that as businessmen we naturally would give them the characteristic "no comment" if we were reached. I noticed that these stories seemed to be filed with the press between five and six p.m. on weekdays or on Sunday afternoon—at both of which times most executives could not be reached or, if they could, were unable to reach their lawyers for advice as to what they should say.

So, as an experiment, I asked to meet with all the cognizant reporters and columnists from the New York press and wire services. I assumed they would nearly all be avid union members and supporters and thus, even on the basis of what they had been reading in their own papers, would be against me ideologically and practically. But their only source of news had been from the unions and their allies, and I thought I should gamble on their being newsmen first and seeing enough value in a business source who would talk on controversial matters to play fair with what I offered them.

Almost all those invited came. I gave them my night phone number at the office and the phone number of a nearby apartment, and told them I could henceforth be reached at one or

UNDER THE CURRENT GE PROPOSAL?

21 GE JOB DIVIDENDS
ADD $700 <u>EXTRA</u> PER YEAR
ABOVE GE PAY CHECKS

REPORT TO EMPLOYEES
ON
NEGOTIATIONS

Our replies to some questions about

CHECK-OFF...
UNION MEMBERSHIP...
STRIKE

We are getting so many inquiries verbally at the individual plants, as well as by mail and phone, that we feel under obligation to repeat here what we have been saying to individual employees who have sought information.

"WHAT'S IT WORTH TO ME?"

(Specimen headlines from articles in employee publications)

the other at any time—including late afternoon and evening weekdays and on Sunday. Incidentally, I didn't realize at the time to what degree this commitment was going to interfere with my wife's and my social life for the next decade.

I asked them to call me for comment whenever we were involved directly or indirectly in any story that came in or in any interview they were going to report. I promised in turn that, no matter how controversial or sensitive the subject, I would give them at once, on the phone, any facts I had or any opinions I thought would be helpful to their accurate and complete reporting. I told them there would be no delay for legal clearance or to reduce my statements to writing; I further said they could quote me.

It may be hard for today's reader to sense the atmosphere of 20 years ago and to realize what a startling proposal this was for its day. My guests seemed incredulous but intrigued, and I was relieved to sense in them none of the too-common union-connected hostility to a businessman talking on such subjects instead of being the silent whipping post and taking his beating.

The next Sunday afternoon I had a call at home from one of those who had been present. I had felt that he basically did not approve of me, but nevertheless believed that he was as reliable as he was competent. So, when he asked the questions he had in mind, I replied frankly and as fully as my information and his interest permitted. I was sure he had been among those at the meeting who were incredulous when he kept reading his notes of my replies back to me and asking me if I was sure it was all right to quote them.

His story the next morning took a full column on the front page of his paper and was continued inside. The wire services had picked it up the night before, and it was not only in other New York papers that Monday but on the front page of at least the 50 dailies from other cities from which we received clippings. To my relief—and that of my associates—there was no misquotation or distortion or slant in any one of them.

This is not to imply that the reporters and editors began supporting us, but it did mark the beginning of a much-improved working relationship with most of the New York press. They were extremely careful to call for comment on stories originating elsewhere, and we saw them individually and as a group throughout the year when they so requested or we had news to offer. We had a "roundup" meeting near the end of each year. We did the same with the Washington press.

Some magazines offered a tougher problem. They were particularly wont to fall for preposterous but juicy charges, to send researchers over to see us on Saturdays or Sundays for verification, and then, when they found they could not develop a supportable story that would be "news" by virtue of its being embarrassing to a big company, they would drop the whole thing. I finally got tired of this and complained to the publishers about it, suggesting that beating business over the head was so common it had become dull. A real man-bites-dog story, I added, would be to report one of these preposterous charges and show that it was false. Needless to say, I got nowhere with this.

But despite the fact that most magazines and city dailies showed a bias in favor of union activities and positions right or wrong, I can recall no case in which I was actually misquoted. I had only one real complaint, which was that we could not seem to get the publications, in selecting from our releases on negotiations and in reporting otherwise on our program to include our assurances to union officials and members that we would change an offer, as we did, whenever it became evident it should be changed in the balanced-best-interests of all concerned. I felt that the continued silent treatment accorded this feature was a little pointed and said so, but to no avail.

Despite notable exceptions to the contrary, our problem with the press in general when I left the field still seemed to be one of getting enough people and their thought-leaders to recognize the fact that business is *the many* and not *the few,* to understand the good that business does, and to understand the protection and enhancement of the usefulness of private business is in the self-interest of everyone. Too many publishers still thought it was "good publishing"—in the sense that it would "sell papers"—not only to give uncritical support to unions but to condemn successful private business when it was right as well as when it was wrong. And too many of their writers did the same thing for ideological reasons. I believed, again, that much of this was, in all fairness, due to long neglect on the part of the businessmen of my generation.

6. *Third Parties:* Outside of the two parties having arrived at the bargaining table so unequal, the next most effective deterrent to any meaningful negotiations was the availability of a third party. Third-party intervention was harmful on two counts:

1. *The usual "something more"—*The third party was presumed to be a representative of the public and thus in a neutral position between the two parties. But not even a majority of the public was neutral; most people still appeared to believe that unions had to be supported right or wrong because they were so weak and deserving—though in fact they had become powerful and politically dominant. And the third parties were part of and servants of that public, and even though many of them sincerely tried to put bias aside and be judicious, both the outside and the subconscious pressures were still present. The record will show that, despite many notable and encouraging exceptions, the union generally would "get something more" when third parties took a hand. The employer commonly assumed—often with good reason—that the third party had entered intentionally or subconsciously on the side of the union and that he thus had to face two adversaries instead of one.

In the case of arbitrators one important reason for this feeling was the widespread impression that—since the power of the unions gave them the determining voice in selections—an arbitrator would be shut off from lucrative assignments if it were found that he did not, on balance, side with the unions.

2. *The irresistable temptation—*It follows from this that the ever-present availability of third-party intervention prevented the two original parties from reaching agreement whenever a union official wanted "more" for political or mistaken ideological reasons, without regard to what would contribute to good jobs. The official in such a case could not realistically be expected to come to agreement at the original bargaining table when the chances seemed so good that any third-party action or influence would be heavily weighted on his side.

In our own case, we had succeeded fairly well in keeping the arbitrable issues relatively few. And since it was our policy to lay everything on the line just as religiously in arbitrable matters as in other aspects of our offers and relations, we did not fare too badly in arbitration except for a few occasions when the arbiter seemed called on to do something just on general principles or for the good of the cause.

But in the other areas of bargaining with some of the more politically minded union officials, we found ourselves more and more in the position of going through all the "musical chairs" that were conceivably available. After weeks of winnowing and cutting and fitting in an effort to develop our offer with as much constructive help as we could get in the face of constantly repeated demands that were so far out of line as hardly to be pertinent at all, we would finally make the offer. The answer would be substantially: "Fine! Now let's bargain for the rest of our demands." After exhausting all possibilities, we would be faced with well-publicized demands for arbitration or mediation by a committee of mayors selected from our plant cities, then by a group of clergymen selected by the union, then by a group of educators, then by a state mediation board, and finally—after the union had apparently failed to get direct White House intervention on the absurd basis that the country's health and safety was endangered or that a "crisis that would bring on chaos" was imminent—the Federal Mediation and Conciliation Service would be called in by the union. Meanwhile, the employees involved would be going undisturbed about their work, waiting for the benefits that many other unions already had accepted for their GE members.

We usually were able to avoid the needless delay in settlement that would have resulted from bringing in the other third parties, but we were compelled by law to accept the services of the Federal and Conciliation Service when the union sent for it and it then asked to intervene. I am sure the reader will by now understand when I say that I had almost always been somewhat nervous and apprehensive when anybody from government became involved in any choice between a claim by a union official and one by a private business manager. However well-intentioned the elected or appointed public servant might be—and I had long contended loudly that the caliber of people in government was far higher than we businessmen and our fellow citizens deserved—I was always conscious of the tremendous pressure on him from people who had been given such great political power by a misled majority of the public.

But however warranted my qualms might have been about others, I certainly had no serious cause for complaint about any of the federal mediators with whom I came in contact. They usually seemed to be appreciative of the thoroughness, scope, and adequacy of our final offer before their intervention, and, while they would occasionally ask if we were sure we couldn't find that "some little something" to serve the union officials' purposes, they were always careful not to put pressure on us to do so.

We did have one bit of unpleasantness, not with any of the mediators themselves but higher up in the service. It occurred in connection with negotiations with two unions which were cooperating in what we—and apparently others, judging by the wire below—viewed as an effort to get the union shop, though the union-shop demand was, as usual, combined with others. This wire of May 7, 1952, is self-explanatory.

Mr. _____
FEDERAL MEDIATION AND CONCILIATION SERVICE
WASHINGTON, D.C.

    WE HAVE YOUR WIRED REQUEST FOR WASHINGTON MEDIATION OF "UNRESOLVED DISPUTES" WITH _____ AT OUR LOCKLAND PLANT NEAR CINCINNATI WHERE WE MAKE ONLY MILITARY JET ENGINES FOR THE UNITED STATES GOVERNMENT.

    WE WILL AS HERETOFORE BE WILLING TO MEET WITH YOU, ALTHOUGH WE UNDERSTAND FULLY THAT THE CURRENT SUBSTITUTE FOR COLLECTIVE BARGAINING IS TO HAVE A FINAL PERFUNCTORY MEDIATION MEETING IN WASHINGTON BEFORE THE UNION HAS ITS CASE CERTIFIED TO THE WAGE STABILIZATION BOARD WHERE IT KNOWS IT CAN SECURE APPROVAL FOR THE UNION SHOP AND UNWARRANTED WAGE SCALE RECOMMENDATIONS, ALL OF WHICH HAS COME TO MAKE ANY NORMAL AND GENUINE COLLECTIVE BARGAINING HARDLY TO BE EXPECTED OF ANY UNION.

    FROM THE OUTSET WE WANT THE RECORD TO BE CLEAR AND THEREFORE CALL YOUR ATTENTION TO THE FOLLOWING FACTS.

YOUR MEDIATORS HAVE MET FREQUENTLY WITH COMPANY AND UNION REPRESENTATIVES AT CINCINNATI DURING THE PAST EIGHT WEEKS. WE KNOW OF NO REASON FOR TRANSFERRING THE MEDIATION MEETINGS FROM CINCINNATI TO WASHINGTON EXCEPT THAT THE UNIONS APPEAR TO BELIEVE THAT IN WASHINGTON THEY CAN AND WILL GET THE NOW CUSTOMARY POLITICAL SUPPORT FOR THEIR UNION SHOP DEMAND AS WELL AS SUPPORT FOR A SPECIAL GOVERNMENT AIRCRAFT WAGE SCALE INEXCUSABLY HIGHER THAN WAGE SCALES FOR SIMILAR WORK ON NON-AIRCRAFT PRODUCTS.

YOUR CINCINNATI MEDIATION REPRESENTATIVES MUST HAVE ADVISED YOU THAT THESE TWO ARE THE ONLY MAJOR ISSUES INVOLVED. ON ALL OTHER ISSUES, WE HAVE OFFERED WHAT APPEAR TO BE ALL PROPER AND FEASIBLE COMPROMISES AND WE BELIEVE THAT, WITH THESE TWO ISSUES ASIDE, AN EARLY AGREEMENT COULD BE REACHED. WE HAVE NO EXPECTATION THAT FURTHER MEDIATION IN WASHINGTON ON THE ISSUES OF THE UNION SHOP AND THE GOVERNMENT AIRCRAFT WAGE SCALE WILL PROVE OF VALUE.

ON THE UNION SHOP ISSUE AT LOCKLAND WE FEEL THAT YOU HAVE DISQUALIFIED YOURSELF AND YOUR ASSOCIATES IN A WAY THAT MAKES IT IMPOSSIBLE FOR YOU TO FUNCTION AS A TRUE AND IMPARTIAL MEDIATION AGENCY. WHEN YOU SPOKE ON THIS SUBJECT SOME TIME BACK TO A HIGH OFFICIAL OF OUR COMPANY, YOU INDICATED YOU HAD ALREADY PRE-JUDGED AND PRE-DETERMINED THIS ISSUE THROUGH STATING THAT YOU PERSONALLY FELT G.E.'S PUBLICLY EXPRESSED POLICY OF OPPOSITION TO COMPULSORY UNION MEMBERSHIP WAS "CHILDISH." YOU URGE THAT WE GIVE IN TO THE UNION ON THE UNION SHOP ISSUE AT LOCKLAND TO AVOID A STRIKE. YOU APPEARED TO FEEL THAT IT WAS PERFECTLY ALL RIGHT FOR THE UNIONS TO CALL A STRIKE BUT ABSOLUTELY ALL WRONG FOR US TO BE PERMITTED TO RESIST IT EVEN IN THE PUBLIC INTEREST. YOU WILL RECALL YOUR SAYING WE WOULD BE "OPENED UP." IN THE LIGHT OF CURRENT EVENTS YOUR STATEMENT COULD HAVE NO OTHER MEANING THAN A THREAT OF GOVERNMENT SEIZURE COMMUNICATED TO US BY A SUPPOSEDLY IMPARTIAL GOVERNMENT AGENCY WHICH NOW PROPOSES TO MEDIATE THE VERY ISSUE ON WHICH IT HAD EXPRESSED SO BIASED A STAND. IN THESE CIRCUMSTANCES, AND SO LONG AS GOVERNMENT CONTINUES ITS ONE-WAY-STREET PRACTICE OF BACKING UNWARRANTED STRIKE THREATS BY TAKING OVER MANAGEMENT, MEDIATION AS WELL AS COLLECTIVE BARGAINING MUST CONTINUE A RATHER FUTILE PROCESS.

ON THE ISSUE OF A SPECIALLY HIGH GOVERNMENT AIR-
CRAFT WAGE SCALE WE FEEL THAT NO AMOUNT OF MEDIA-
TION SHOULD OR COULD INDUCE US TO AGREE TO PAY WAGES
WHICH ARE IN EXCESS OF THE TRADITIONAL AND ESTAB-
LISHED COMMUNITY PATTERN IN CINCINNATI. EVEN THOUGH
THE COST OF THE HIGHER RATES, WITH POSSIBLE MINOR
EXCEPTIONS, WOULD BE PAID FOR BY THE GOVERNMENT AND
NOT G.E., WE FEEL WE HAVE A MORAL OBLIGATION TO THE
GOVERNMENT AND TO THE NATION'S TAXPAYERS TO MAIN-
TAIN THIS POSITION. WE SEE NO ETHICAL OR MORAL REASONS
WHICH JUSTIFY A DIFFERENCE IN PAY BETWEEN MEN WITH
THE SAME SKILL DOING THE SAME WORK MERELY BECAUSE
ONE IS BEING PAID BY OUR GOVERNMENT IN A PERIOD OF
DISTRESS WHILE THE OTHER IS BEING PAID BY PRIVATE
PARTIES. THE VERY ASSERTION OF THIS CLAIM CAN BE
NOTHING OTHER THAN AN ATTEMPT TO CAPITALIZE AND
TRADE UPON OUR COUNTRY'S DANGER. THE HIGH GOVERN-
MENT AIRCRAFT WAGES ORIGINATED DURING THE CRITICAL
MAN-POWER SHORTAGE OF THE LAST WORLD WAR WHEN
THERE WAS AN URGENT NEED TO ATTRACT WORKERS INTO
THE AIRCRAFT INDUSTRY. THAT SITUATION DOES NOT EXIST
TODAY AT LOCKLAND.

EXPERIENCE SHOWS, MOREOVER, THAT RATES IN A DE-
FENSE PLANT WILL INEVITABLY SPREAD TO OTHER NON-
DEFENSE BUSINESSES BOTH LARGE AND SMALL. WAGES ALONE
IN OUR LOCKLAND PLANT HAVE ALREADY GONE UP AN
AVERAGE OF 34 CENTS AN HOUR SINCE THE JANUARY 1950
W.S.B. BASE DATE AND WE ARE CURRENTLY OFFERING AN
ADDITIONAL WAGE INCREASE OFFSETTING THE RISE IN THE
COST OF LIVING FOR THE LAST SIX MONTHS. WE DO NOT WANT
TO BE A PARTY TO ANY GOVERNMENT-UNION PROGRAM
WHICH USES DEFENSE WORK AS A MEANS OF ARTIFICIALLY
INFLATING THE WAGE PATTERN IN A GIVEN AREA. AN INEX-
CUSABLY HIGH GOVERNMENT AIRCRAFT WAGE SCALE WOULD
RESULT IN HIGHER COSTS OF GROCERIES AND MOST OTHER
COST-OF-LIVING ITEMS IN THE CINCINNATI VICINITY. IT
WOULD ALSO DO VIOLENCE TO THE BASIC PRINCIPLES OF THE
WAGE STABILIZATION BOARD THAT WAGES ARE TO BE DETER-
MINED IN THE LIGHT OF AREA PATTERNS AND SKILLS IN-
VOLVED.

YOUR SUGGESTED DATE OF MAY 12 CONFLICTS WITH
PRIOR ARRANGEMENTS BUT WE COULD BE THERE ON THURS-
DAY OR FRIDAY OF NEXT WEEK. MEANWHILE, WE HAVE MADE
THE FOREGOING STATEMENT IN ORDER THAT NEITHER YOU
NOR OTHERS INTERESTED WILL ENTERTAIN ANY FALSE HOPES
OR EXPECTATIONS AS TO THE POSSIBILITY THAT SUCH MEDIA-
TION MEETINGS WOULD BE PROFITABLE INSOFAR AS THEY

RELATE TO THE UNION SHOP ISSUE AND ANY SPECIAL GOV-
ERNMENT AIRCRAFT WAGE SCALE. THESE ARE NO MORE THAN
THE VIEWS WHICH WE HAVE ALREADY COMMUNICATED TO
MEDIATION REPRESENTATIVES IN CINCINNATI AND WE WOULD
INTEND TO ADHERE TO THEM IN ANY MEETINGS IN WASHING-
TON.

L. R. BOULWARE

On the morning we arrived in Washington to start what we
guessed would be a protracted series of mediation meetings, we
ran the above wire in full—with some brief explanatory text—in
full-page advertisements in the four Washington newspapers under
the heading "LET'S SEE HOW THIS ONE COMES OUT." We had
in mind that Congress was in session, and that the information we
offered might be quite educational.

Just after we had all assembled for the first session—with all
three mediators busy reading our page in one of the papers—they
were called away and were gone all day, phoning us later that they
would meet with us the next day. We ran full-page ads in all the
papers the next day with a very brief report of the previous day's
events under the heading: "NOTHING HAPPENED YESTER-
DAY—LET'S SEE WHAT DOES TODAY."

When the mediators arrived the next morning, they again were
almost immediately called away. They soon returned to express
the opinion that Washington furnished a poor atmosphere at that
time for settlement of the dispute and that we should return to
bargaining between the two parties at Cincinnati. I jokingly told
the three mediators—who obviously were the usual good folks but
in an embarrassing position—that we did not want to go home but
wanted to stay and run the rest of our ads. But we, of course,
went home. There was another brief mediation session at our
offices in New York in about two weeks with no change in
position by either side, and, after another set of meetings between
the two parties at Cincinnati, settlement was reached on the offer
exactly as developed in negotiations prior to all the commotion.

In contrast to the agreeable surprise of receiving such
relatively fair treatment by most federal mediators as individuals,
our experiences with the National Labor Relations Board and the
so-called "Labor" Department confirmed the worst fears I had
acquired in my Washington service and from my subsequent

observations. Both these agencies seemed most of the time to take it for granted that they were there to act first and foremost as agents of the union officials even when this was contrary to the interests of workers or the balanced interests of the citizenry generally. Both seemed to be regarded by the politicians in power as payoff points for past political support by the union officials and as channels of prepayment for support in future elections.

The Wagner Act's initial concept—of making the NLRB, despite the camouflage, advocate, judge, and jury all rolled into one—was completely wrong by every theory and experience developed over man's long struggle for fairness before his government. And the current experience was confirming this all over again day after day and year after year. The NLRB was so openly biased in favor of union officials' own purposes—right or wrong—that I could not believe the public could continue to tolerate the obvious abuse of worker wishes and the common interest. But in my time the public never became aware that its own ox was being gored, so Congress quite naturally kept on looking the other way.

The Department of Labor was a particular problem at times, and perhaps I was unfair in feeling so strongly as I did on the subject, but my few experiences with it led me to conclude each time that it, too, was representing primarily the union officials rather than union members or other workers or the public. As union members constituted only one fourth to one fifth of the work force, I once recommended that the existing agency be called the Department of Union Labor, and that a separate department be set up—three or four times as large—to serve the interests of the three quarters or four fifths of the work force that had stayed out of unions despite the enormously powerful and "persuasive" pressures on workers from unions and government to join. What had been going on—in addition to this rank unfairness to the majority of workers—appeared to be a political contradiction of the first order. Our government's eager and lavish assistance to "small business"—not only in financing but also, and especially, in righting any actual or fancied inequality of opportunity with "big" business—had seemed to supply an obvious precedent of the soundest political significance. Politics is a game of numbers, and it had proved to be "good politics" to take care of the many interested in "small" business rather than what was erroneously believed to be the few interested in "big" business. Thus it surely would be "good politics" for candidates and office holders to concern themselves with the rights and opportunities of so-called "small labor" more than with those of "big labor," especially when the "smalls" represented four or five times as many votes as the "bigs."

19 PUBLIC OPINION

To repeat again, the whole purpose of our program was to earn and obtain the cooperation of our employees and neighbors in directions that would be genuinely in their own interests and thus inescapably—with our private business system—in the interests of all the other contributor-claimants, too.

I have given a disproportionate amount of space to my views on what seemed to me to be the political character of so much of the activity of union officials and their allies. They spent billions of dollars of employee, government, and other money from the public in supporting politicians who so often played upon the ignorance of their constituents instead of helping them to correct their misinformation, misconceptions, or just plain lack of information. One of my serious hopes was to help make a start toward an informed electorate which would permit both union and government politicians to talk and act more sensibly for the real good of those they represented.

But all this has been recounted not as a mere exposure of what went on then but as an additional illustration of how many and varied and surprising were the places where obstacles to employee and community cooperation were to be found. In this connection, it is important to note that, with union membership staying at around 15 or 16 million while the work force was about doubling, union power over business and government resulted more and more from the expenditure of the time and money of members to spread "education" and to elect friends and defeat enemies. In short, political support came increasingly from the public at the ballot box and decreasingly from the members at the union hall.

This is perhaps taking the long way around to demonstrate again that, after all possible had been done with the employee at work, our major effort still remained with him, his family, and the rest of the public—near and far—as citizens. In the final analysis, the chief concern of a private business—not only in job-connected matters but in all other areas where appreciation and cooperation were needed—seemed to be in the public's opinion about private business.

It seemed to us all along that a frontal assault across the whole country could not be made on the prevailing misinformation about private business. If there was to be a correction, it would have to come from the cumulative efforts of individual thought-leaders in individual communities. So we kept reminding and urging our managers in over 140 locations that each must do his individual part in the twin hope that this not only would do good by itself but also would encourage and reinforce others in working toward the same end in their own ways.

The following is one of the typical messages on this subject which were sent to all our managers and known community thought-leaders. It makes up the whole of the *Employee Relations News Letter* of June 3, 1955.

The Community's Problem in
GETTING AND KEEPING GOOD EMPLOYERS

We Want to Help

We are impressed with the number of requests we get for information as to what a community has to do to attract and keep a good employer. They come from our managers, from other leaders among our employees, and from our neighbors in the communities where we operate.

These requests indicate a new and pressing community interest in getting and keeping the successful type of employer whose sales bring in the money that breeds prosperity as it goes through many sets of hands in the community and who, in the process, provides the steadiest and most rapidly expanding jobs possible.

This new and urgent interest seems to spread pretty well across the whole of the old industrial area north of the Ohio and east of the Mississippi where we have more than 81% of our plants and more than 90% of our employment. Interest in getting and keeping good employers seems to be most acute in Massachusetts and New York where more than 4 out of 10 of our employees are located, and where a vast variety of costs, in addition to those for wages, have become alarmingly high as compared to those in most of the other 46 states.

We are vitally interested in being able to continue to stay in all of these old areas which so many others have been leaving. As loyal citizens of the communities in which our plants are located, we are disturbed by mounting evidence that many of them have lost much of their power to attract and keep good employers. We want to do our part to make it possible for the native skills and acquired know-how of our own employees and of our neighbors in these locations to continue to be utilized among home surroundings.

One of the things that will most help us be able to stay is to have other successful employers come and stay in these old communities where we are trying to continue to operate. There are two reasons for this. The first is that they will share the tax and other such community costs and will supply a needed diversity of employment opportunities. The second reason is that the willingness of successful employers to stay there will be evidence in itself that the community is remaining or becoming a rewarding place in which to operate and live.

We also want our vast investment there to be preserved and enhanced in value—whereas that investment will be *worthless* if we and others find it impossible to *operate at a profit* there.

Thus-quite aside from our loyalty to these communities and our desire to be a good corporate citizen in each of them over and beyond any normal call of duty-we have a very substantial reason for wanting to help thesy communities in their current efforts to attract and keep other employers besides ourselves.

What Will Help?

In reply to requests as to how communities may accomplish this job of attracting and keeping good employers, we have only been able to relate what it is we in General Electric are trying to get done at a given location and how the community can help. We simply assume that what we are trying to do—and what we need to help us do it—are characteristic of the efforts and needs of other conscientious employers a community might want to try to attract and keep.

We are accordingly repeating the summary below on the assumption that the rest of you are just as interested as those managers and others who have already requested our suggestions.

Two-Way Relationship

We are a customer of the community. As in any other free-market relationship between customer and supplier, this one will not work successfully for *either* party for long unless it is a two-way, value-received, something-for-*something* arrangement that is *mutually* rewarding. *Both* the community and we have got to *give* as well as *receive*.

This employer-community relationship cannot, of course, be treated as separate from and unrelated to our over-all relationships. Our mission in General Electric is to please people at a profit through doing what they want us to do in bringing together the necessary contributions and settling the resulting proper claims of the five sets of contributor-claimants; i.e., the customers, owners, suppliers, employees, and community-neighbors or the more distantly involved public. If we are to succeed in our mission for the good of all concerned, these contributions and claims have to be settled in the balanced best interests of all five—even if there were not the great overlap that now makes each contributor-claimant appear usually in at least three of these roles and sometimes in all five.

What the Community Will Find
General Electric Trying to Do

There are a number of objectives which we try constantly to meet in carrying on our activities in the various communities where our plants are located.

We sometimes fail, of course, in our efforts to live up to the standards we have set for ourselves. Despite occasional failures, however, we want to keep on trying at all times to provide these things in our plant communities:

1. *Good Products.*—We produce top quality goods and provide top quality service not only to get local customers but to attract and hold distant customers whose payments, when brought into the community, go through several sets of hands in the community before going outside to buy things the community wants brought in.

2. *Good Jobs.*—We try at all times to be a good employer of local folks—with good pay in return for good work ... good human relations *both* ways between managers and employees ... good information, education, participation, opportunity, and other material and spiritual rewards from the important and exciting assignments we are carrying out together in our warm association there.

3. *Good Purchases.*—We make a conscious and continuous effort to be a good customer for the goods and services of local suppliers—with one of our most valuable and socially significant contributions being the taking on of all sorts of big assignments and then breaking them up into the size or kind of jobs that can be performed by our 40,000 large and small suppliers, most of whom are quite naturally to be found in the communities where we operate plants.

4. *Good Citizenship.*—We will be found trying at all times in the community to be a good corporate citizen—such, for instance, as being a good taxpayer with no bargains asked; a good supporter of local charities (first, by generous contributions, and second, by our good pension, insurance and other employee benefit programs which insure that we will be no drain on these local charities); and a good worker in all other worth-while activities aimed at making the community a rewarding place in which to operate, work and live. Incidentally, besides our corporate activity, our individual managers and other employees are encouraged in their own desires to be useful individual citizens of the communities in which they live and work.

5. *Good Loyalty.*—At all times we try to be warmly loyal to the good people, good institutions, and good projects in the community. Where it is a matter of our proper concern, we will carry this loyalty to the point of disagreeing publicly, as a matter of duty, with those who seem to be speaking or working contrary to the over-all community interest.

6. *Good Profit.*—We try to maintain a profitable operation in the community in order to promote the strength and growth of our activity there and to reward properly the more than 300,000 share owners who risk their savings to supply us with facilities and backing to make jobs possible there in the first place. All employees there have an opportunity to become share owners under our savings and stock bonus plan, and it has been gratifying to note the increasing number of our community-neighbors who have been choosing to invest their savings with us.

What General Electric Needs From the Community

The number and steadiness of the jobs we can bring to a community—and the size and steadiness of the flow of money we can bring to all concerned in that community—depend on our ability to be competitive while satisfying all the just claims of the various contributors.

Our ability to remain competitive depends in turn upon how our costs of doing business compare to the costs which our many competitors incur in other locations.

There are a hundred-and-one costs which can and do vary widely from one community to another. Some of the more important cost disadvantages which, especially when they occur together, may discourage employers from locating in or staying in a particular area are: local and state taxes which bear unfairly upon a business, are administered in a discriminatory fashion, or become disproportionately or unbearably high as a result of extravagant government spending; unemployment compensation abuses which, for example, keep costs high by providing payments for reasons other than actual lack of work; workmen's compensation abuses such as administration that fails to distinguish between the honest injury and the exaggerated claim; featherbedding and spread-the-work schemes which reduce output and thus increase production costs; organized resistance to improved machines and methods; slow-downs, walk-outs, and improper strikes; illegal picketing which is permitted by some public servants who may think that inaction in this matter is "good politics"; labor laws which either fail to protect the interests of employees, employers, and the public, or are administered in a one-sided fashion; community tolerance of illegal union boycotts; inflated construction costs; and unfavorable effects on productivity and on customer patronage arising from unfair and abusive treatment in politically-inspired investigations, inquiries, and hearings, or from misguided support when given by the press, educators, clergy, public servants and others of influence to unwarranted attacks on local employers.

It is obvious from this listing of some types of cost disadvantages, as well as from other evidence, that many of the old industrial communities have a tough competitive problem now and ahead. They have got to offset some natural and acquired disadvantages by performing brilliantly in the other areas which are still open to them for improvement.

Yet we can expect a community to do for us in the end only what the local citizens believe is in the short and long term best interest of the community. We know the community can do for us only what is in fair return for what we do there in the over-all community interest.

What then are the things we need from a community in order that we can survive there and, in the process, operate in the interests of the community as well as all others concerned? They are just the same things we believe the community *should be trying* to supply in *fair return* for the contributions we make. Here are some of the things we look for:

1. *Basic Ingredients.*—We watch the number and skill of the potential employees available; existing local and connecting transportation facilities; power, fuel, and water supply; available housing and plant sites; educational, recreational, religious and cultural facilities.

2. *Success Record.*—We watch whether other employers are being successful there. If not, is it the fault of the employer or the community? If plants have been empty there for some time, why hasn't the high cost of building new plants elsewhere made these empty ones attractive buys?

3. *Business Climate.*—We watch to see whether we can expect understanding, respect, and fair treatment, *where we deserve it,* from the community's public servants in such areas, for instance, as the courts, taxes, and law enforcement.

This is a matter of growing importance as a result of the way so many communities in recent years have been increasingly allowing their public servants to practice, as "good politics," the strangling of the industrial goose that lays the golden eggs of local prosperity—by such things as discriminatory taxation, unwise zoning or building ordinances, or even by choosing to *protect law breakers* in their brutal abuses of the persons and property of peaceful, *law-abiding* citizens.

Fortunately, these situations can be and often have been remedied through community leaders helping their community get—
  ... economic education to help all concerned know what is the right thing to be done in their own interests and in the balanced best interests of all;
  ... moral reawakening to help all concerned with a determination to see that such right thing is done voluntarily;

What Do We Seek?

And how much of that is in our own hands?

Two Cars In Every Garage?

WHY DO OUR BEST?

Getting Along Together

DOING OUR PART TOGETHER

(Specimen headlines and illustration from employee publications)

. . . political sophistication to guard all concerned against being bribed or fooled by demagogs.

4. *Competitive Costs.*—We watch to see if competitive costs are causing *old* employers to go out of business or to do their expanding in less oppressive areas. We check to see if *new* employers have been eager or reluctant to locate in the community on account of the cost possibilities from local or state influences. As already seen, excessive costs of operation arise from many important sources other than high wage rates; so, whether it is a high wage area or not, we check to see *if all concerned are cooperating* in other available ways to keep total production costs competitive. We check also to see if attempts are being made to mask local cost disadvantages by politically-inspired subsidies or by other unsound political means. Temporary tax or other such advantages are of little or no interest when one is seriously seeking a permanent location in which to try to operate profitably and expand over the years. Being lured into a situation—and then beaten to death over the years—is not the kind of promising or "considered" risk on which management has any license to put up investors' savings.

The cost of carrying on a business in one place as compared to another is of prime importance when an employer is trying to decide where to locate. Once an employer is established in a particular community, of course, he is reluctant to move even when costs of doing business there start to get out of line. Eventually, however, employers located in communities which develop sizeable cost disadvantages that threaten to price them out of the market, must either go out of business or move to some other location.

This question of *competitive costs* is the central one—and the other considerations covered above only add to or detract from the problem. Both the community and the employer have the same competitive cost problem—i.e., costs must be kept well within the selling price or there will be no jobs and only empty factories. But the community has the tougher role of the two—for it has no choice of locations but must succeed or fail at the *one* location. And what a community must do, where it has wage and other cost disadvantages, is to try to offset these by effective application of employee skill, care, and effort; by embracing and not resisting technological advances; but cutting out featherbedding and other cost-raising practices like those previously listed; and by having it "good politics" to protect and encourage, *where deserved*, the community's bread-winning employers.

5. *Community Loyalty.*—We watch to see if the thought leaders and other representatives in the community speak well of the *deserving* employers there or consider them whipping posts. Spokesmen for unions and other organizations, as well as invididuals among clergy-man, teachers, politicians, and publishers can all have a very material

effect for good or bad on the *cost of producing* goods and on the *amount and regularity* of the *sale* of those goods. A little noted fact is that public criticism of an employer—to the extent it is believed—tends to cut down jobs for employees. Likewise—understanding, approval and warranted public praise of an employer tend to cut his costs and increase his sales—*and jobs.*

Just as total traffic can be much more than doubled by replacing a single-lane road with a two-lane highway, so community well-being can be greatly increased by developing a genuine two-way "something-for-something" relationship between employers and the community. In the future, as in the past, we believe our managers and other leading employees will remain eager to contribute their time and energy to making the community a better place in which to live. These efforts, on our part, and those of other employers, will be only partly successful, however, unless community leaders match these contributions by imaginative, zealous and continuous efforts to make their community an attractive place in which to operate a business.

EMPLOYEE AND PLANT COMMUNITY
RELATIONS SERVICES

20 WHOSE JOB

In case any reader may still feel I have been too tough on other people of influence, let me say once again that I believed all along that the primary responsibility for the resistance to cooperation which was so limiting the usefulness of private business lay finally with the business manager and the business owner.

To be sure, it was not the manager's or the rich man's ox that was being gored; it was the whole public's ox. However, the public—from whom the authority and insistence for any correction had to come—was being prevented from getting the information required for such corrective action simply because it was continuing to depend on the wrong kind of thought-leaders. It would have to be persuaded to shift to better thought-leaders if it was to save itself from the inevitable consequences of the something-for-nothing course.

Normally, educators would be showing up the bad arithmetic and bad economics of the scheme. Normally, the clergy would be denouncing the bad morals of a willingness even to try for something-for-nothing. But the public was getting all too little help from these sources. And the other usually independent thought-leaders were too often going along unthinkingly with the tide.

So, while it had too long been considered not our job, I thought the time had come when only we managers were left to do the job and that we simply had to come clean with all our contributor-claimants—that is, with any and all in the public—by explaining clearly how the false teachings were limiting what private business could deliver in the material and nonmaterial ways.

To the Harvard Business School alumni during the 1949 commencement I had delivered an exhortation on the subject of the businessman being largely to blame for the fix we were in and the only one who could do anything to start the correction. I was asked to repeat this "salvation is not free" address at the Chicago and Detroit Economic Clubs and before 17 other business meetings or conventions in the next few months, and many thousands of printed copies were distributed by these organizations in addition to the many thousands we ourselves sent to our employees and neighbors.

I cite this distribution and quote a substantial part of the address below to underscore two points. One is that, while I may have seemed overly critical of others and felt they could have been doing more despite the trend of public opinion, my real complaint was not against them but against us businessmen who, having had the abuses of the public interest right under our noses, had not taken the necessary lead toward correction. The other point I want to stress is that we did not confine these exhortations to our own plants or even our own communities but went outside to try to persuade other businessmen and other thought-leaders to get busy on what was a needed—a possible, and a most rewarding, job.

Here are some excerpts from the 1949 speech which may still be significant:

SALVATION IS NOT FREE

. . . . Every one of you must already be a pronounced success in your business or profession—successful in what has long been thought was the principal, and maybe only, field activity for which society held you individually responsible.

But I assume you share my embarrassed realization that we here—and others like us everywhere—must not have been doing our whole duty.

What's the evidence we—and too many other like us—have not been doing this whole duty?

The evidence is clear. It's the too-common economic illiteracy among us businessmen, among our employees and their families and neighbors, and among the representatives of all of us in government, in unions, in education, in the clergy, and elsewhere.

Too many of us just do not understand how we got this standard of living that's the envy of the rest of the world.

Too many of us working, and buying, and voting adults just don't understand the parts played by the customer, the worker, the manager, as well as the saver . . . that each of these has a necessary part to play, but not one of them can play it, or will even try, unless the incentive is there, unless he thinks he is going to get what's right from the others for what he does.

The penalty for such economic ignorance can be—is already—very great in both the economic and political fields. Our free markets and our free persons are at stake.

We don't like the proposals for further greatly enlarged government expenditures now being urged on the public by a combination of government and union officials.

The size of taxes—now and proposed—is bad enough.

But the manner of their collection is disgracefully worse—is infinitely more ominous for our whole future as well as for the future of any free market and any free person—for our taxes are now being based on political rather than economic considerations.

We see all this unsound program being misrepresented, "sold" to the public, if you will—by the public's own representatives in government and in unions—as though it were a free service by a great and wealthy and indulgent government. And we see our government keep trying to give the impression to the vast majority of citizens that it can get the money from somebody else—right while the costs of the current so-called "free" benefits are at the very moment being taken directly and indirectly out of the pockets of the whole public—from you and me—from all our employees—from everybody.

The costs are being collected from everybody in the taxes the government hides in consumer prices . . . in the inflation, from deficit spending and unsound monetary practices, which also turn right up in consumer prices . . . in the prices that are higher than they would be, even under these circumstances, if it had not become "the thing to do" to tax unfairly, and otherwise to be hostile to, the income and savings of the very people who would finance more arm-lengthening equipment and methods to make bigger real values available in every store.

Despite these real causes, we see the profits and other supposed inhumanities of businessmen or their corporations all the while being blamed for high prices—for supposedly keeping the worker from getting back more of what he produces.

There are other things we don't like—other things that are frightening—in the public's misinformation and consequent vulnerability to current economic and political demagoguery.

We all believe, of course, that good unions are possible and have a useful function they can perform in the employee and public interest. We have had ample evidence of how wise government representatives can promote that free play of incentives and rewards which brings a higher standard of living.

But we are horrified at the way representatives, both in government and in unions, so frequently say and do things they—as well as we—know to be economically unsound.

We can hardly believe our eyes when we see the platforms of our two major parties incorporating just about the same unsound economics—just about the same something-for-nothing promises.

There seems never, never any honest explanation that all of us pay the bill, and pay it soon, if not immediately. We've got to learn that—in government programs as elsewhere—there isn't any such thing as "a free lunch." I think we have maybe got to get something like the Better Business Bureau after our office holders and politicians—low and high—in all parties.

If it were not for what we see along this line over here in America, we would be hard-put to explain why the British Conservative Party platform for next year is so shockingly close to being economically the same as the British Socialist Labor Party platform.

The plain fact is that most all politicians in all parties and all lands—no matter what their private convictions on economic matters— think that the majority of adults everywhere are so misinformed that they not only believe "something-for-nothing" is really possible, but demand it. They think the public just would not understand or support them if they spoke and acted soundly.

Hence so many public leaders openly espouse and support unsound schemes. For years, from within our own government has come a persistent endorsement and following of such unsound and demagogic ideas—so much so as to be an actual attack from within on the very free economic and political system our officials are sworn to defend and protect. You all may know—as I do—government and union officials who are appalled, even frightened, at what they find themselves saying and doing in order to fit in with public ignorance of economic facts.

But I suspect our greatest consternation—our deepest distress of all—is over the low estate in which we businessmen find ourselves before our employees and the public.

Here we are—with incredible achievements to show for our management of the business side of our wonderful system of freedoms, incentives, and competition.

We are great physicists, chemists, engineers. We are phenomenal manufacturers. We have been fabulous financiers. We are superb in individual selling and mass marketing.

People like—and respect—the results of our separate professional skills.

But taken as the whole man of business, each of us is too likely to be condemned by a majority of the public as anti-social. We always seem to be coldly against everything—never seem to know clearly what are the good objectives we *claim* to be seeking—never seem to be willing or able to speak up warmly and convincingly to prove that what we are doing is for the common good.

As a result, too many of our employees and too many of their friends and representatives—in unions, in government, among educators and clergy, in the whole public—in other words too many of our real bosses—not only do not respect us but also do not like us. They do not understand or appreciate what we are trying to do. And let's be frank about it—there are times when it looks like *we* don't, either.

Too many people just don't think that the jobs we provide are what they ought to be. They don't think that the economic and social consequences of our activities, and the system back of our activities, are what they ought to be for the good of each community and of the nation.

They do not even credit us with good intentions toward them—with being on their side—whereas we thoroughly believe that being on their side is being on the side of what's good for all.

They even doubt our honesty and competence in this broader economic and social field—where they have been led to believe some magic, some escape from the rules of arithmetic, is possible.

Hence, our participation is not sought—or even tolerated—in important public affairs.

It has become popular, and therefore politically expedient, to heap injustices upon us, and even to put limitations on our carrying out what people want us to do for them.

Yet we are the same people who give those very folks, who distrust us, the products and prices and responsible guarantees which they have proved they trust and like—proved in the hundreds of millions of individual instances of daily customer preferences in millions of separate free markets.

We have got to admit that our business system and our businessmen have produced a fantastic fairyland of well-being . . . . especially when we think of the new burdens we are carrying and when we think of what is now, or has ever been, possible anywhere else in the world. But people are being taught to look right at this and not see it—to see something different and *bad*.

How do people all over the world get this way? Why do they reject businessmen, who have a fine record of raising the standard of living through voluntary action inspired by the incentive to save and to compete? Why do so many choose, instead, the government planners—with their promises of security and plenty but with their history of skimming off for state purposes everything above a bare subsistence standard of living—and with their inevitable necessity in the end, directly or indirectly, of having to shut off free choice and free speech in order that their planning failures will be masked?

This can only be the fault of us businessmen ourselves. We have been looking right at this new kind of robber barons who have gotten more and more successful elsewhere out around the world during the last thirty years. They always get themselves cloaked in the mantle of the common man. But their objective is power—and power direct rather than through money. Their methods are therefore political and not commercial.

Businessmen, unthinkingly continuing to devote themselves purely to the customary commercial pursuits, where their only skill has been, have meanwhile in country after country been gradually weakened and then displaced. Along with their displacement went freedom—for all the people—freedom and any hope of human dignity, plenty, and the good life.

This can only prove that just too pitifully few businessmen had the alertness to know when they were pushed beyond the commercial field into the political arena. And when they did awaken to their state, too few businessmen seemingly had the courage, or intelligence, or energy to go about correcting misinformation and teaching sound economics.

Yet when most businessmen face essentially this exact type of spurious emotional attacks and something-for-nothing appeals in the commercial field, they have no trouble or the slightest hesitancy in dealing with them devastatingly.

We businessmen are bold and imaginative before commercial competitors.

We are cowardly and silent in public when confronted with union and other economic and political doctrines contrary to our beliefs.

Incidentally, a distinguished professor recently told me that he was beginning to believe that the missing ingredient in the businessman's employee relations, community relations, and public relations is summed up in the one word "politics"—not *party* politics, of course, but private and public political action by managers, farmers, stockholders, bond holders, insurance policy holders, savings bank depositors, pensioners, and any other upstanding citizens with an interest in keeping the value of money honest, the standard of living rising, and the freedom of choice, speech, worship, and movement really free—in other words, the insistence by citizens on the mastery of sound economics by themselves and then on sound economic teaching and practices by their representatives in government, in unions, even in education and the clergy, as well as in business.

We have got to get just as aroused and just as active about all kinds of socialists as we are about the communist brand of socialist. Our real danger is that, while we are scared to death of communism, too many of us seemingly haven't even come to fear socialism at all. The intentions of communists are, of course, the ultimate in the wrong direction. But the potentialities for evil of the socialists—who are careful not to be known as such—are just out of this world, and simply because we are not alerted at all.

Fortune sagely points out that "a democratic government can corrupt an unvigilant people" because of the failure of "so many of its citizens to act on or even fully understand two basic, timeless facts:

1. In the long run the government can give them only what it takes out of their pockets, and

2. Sometimes the government may seem to be doing many of them good when it is only debauching and corrupting them all."

. . . . A vivid but hard lesson that's right at the core of what we have got to learn about representation in government and unions and other organizations—is that leaders are just not often leaders any more. They are followers. They do, and are supposed to do, what the folks back home—or the people represented—want done, regardless of the ignorance that prompts those wants.

If we want bad—or even good—leaders to do what is right economically and politically, we must see that a majority of us, *as citizens at the grass roots,* know what is right economically, do what is accordingly right within the area of our own economic and political activities, and then get and stay forcefully articulate—in private and public—in getting our representatives in government, unions, and elsewhere to act with economic and political horse-sense.

Let's keep in mind that communism and socialism have only recently—and erroneously—come to be thought of by the public as two different things. Communism is just a slight variant of socialism, as were facism and nazism, and is now the British type which is just communism a little less brutal, a little more gentlemanly yet, and in not so much of a hurry.

Our great problem in this country—and the world—is to learn the economic fallacies of the whole socialist theory—and then to act accordingly to keep people from being fooled and pauperized and silenced and enslaved, and to keep our great nation—as we know and love it—from going on the ash-heap of history.

A really free people can live well materially and spiritually where there is the incentive to work, create, compete, save, invest, and profit.

But there must be either force to *drive* men to work. Or there must be incentive to make men *want* to work.

It's "the carrot or the stick"—now, as in all history of man or other animal. And that applies to each of us right here in this room.

People that start out free—with no force over them, but also with no incentive—will starve in any organized society having a subdivision of effort—any society except in that modern-times impossible one where each person serves all his own wants.

Let's watch our British friends to see what happens in their experiment. Probably the only thing that can save British socialism is for us in America to stay strong enough to keep helping them—for us not to debilitate ourselves by continuing our drift into that same socialism. In other words, the recipients of free drinks in this international barroom of socialism have got to see that the American bartender doesn't become a drunk, too.

Meanwhile, what do we have to do to be saved here? What can management do to promote sound economic understanding and resulting sound public action?

We have simply got to learn, and preach, and practice what's the good alternative to socialism. And we have to to interpret this to a majority of adults in a way that is understandable and credible and attractive.

What we have to do is to show the worker and farmer and other citizen that profitable, competitive business does more for him now, and offers the promise of more of the things he wants in the future, than do any of the unsound substitutes being put forward.

So what we really have to do is only just exactly, and faithfully, and every bit as we do when we encounter any other unfair or dishonest salesman out with an unsound product trying to compete for our good customer's favor.

In fact, I'll bet all you honorable and experienced businessmen here hope for no greater blessing than that your competitors will show up as liars and with bad products.

You know that a few—or many—customers may be fooled for a while. But you also know that if you keep your product honest, and if you keep warmly plugging the truth to those customers, you will keep most of them and soon get the rest back.

We have become sophisticated in the product field—we don't expect to get something for nothing or, as businessmen, to have to offer it. Millions of man-days of hard and honest selling have done that for us.

We have become just as sensible and sophisticated in the field of morals. A few husbands will fall for the harlots, but about 99.44 percent of the time the wife today triumphs over the mistress. That's the triumph of millions upon millions of character lessons taught at the mother's knee, or at church, or in the hard knocks of life.

With triumphs like these—in the very difficult fields of products and morals—to show what we can do when we really try, there is just no sense in our having the slighest hesitancy in taking on the selling of whatever our study together teaches us to be the sound, and honest, and good, and richly rewarding economic program that's really the one for us all here in America.

Just as in the case of any parents facing up finally to telling the truth about Santa Claus, we are quite likely to be worse off in some quarters before beginning to be better off.

Even if the employee—and his family and neighbors—feel he has got the best pay, best working conditions, and best boss in town—if he feels his boss and company have been literally "born again," are on his side, and are really putting human considerations first—it still isn't enough.

He goes into the grocery or other store, finds prices that seem outlandishly high. In a flash, this seems to confirm a lot he has been told—told by the agents of those very ones who have been doing the diluting of the money and causing the high prices while blaming businessmen.

He concludes that the grocer—and his own boss back at the shop—are the representatives of a system that is not being operated by people on his side, but by people who are against him—who are maybe even exploiting him, as claimed.

His family and neighbors are too likely to conclude the same.

Unfortunately, the facts will not speak for themselves in this area any more than they will in the commercial area. The facts have got first to be good—but then they have got to be constantly pointed out and explained and repeated to him—just as the commercial customer has to be both initially sold and then kept constantly reminded.

For us to accomplish this—and have a favorable climate for our further operations—the public has got to be helped to understand the rudiments of sound economics, and then the public has got to have itself and its representatives be guided by the sound principles of economics so learned.

This is a big and hard job. But we think it can be done, and that it's got to be done if business management—in fact, of our free system of incentives and competition—is to survive.

But this is no job for *one* company or for the employers and other good citizens in a *few* communities. It's the job for every businessman—every citizen—to go back to school on economics individually, in small groups, in big groups . . . to learn from simple text books, from organized courses, from individual discussions with business associates, in neighborhood groups, at the club or bar, on the train or bus.

Let's learn again that socialism is just communism in not so *much* of a hurry—but in *quite* a hurry.

Let's appreciate again how silence and lack of sophistication by us businessmen and other free enterprisers in the last thirty years have guaranteed the coming of the things that now terrify us.

Let's consider the tragedy—and the peril—in how pitifully few of us in management at the moment are really competent to do anything about it—have the energy and courage to be even trying!

The current rapid trend has got to be changed, or we are through with every good thing we cherish.

And we businessmen have got to do the job. It will not be done by others—we are the only ones left to do it.

So—let's do it.

Let's here at this moment covenant together that we ourselves—without waiting for any others—are now individually going to make the start .... that we are each going to study until we understand this wonderful system of ours .... that we are going to find out how to preserve and improve it rather than let it be damaged or even perish along with our free market and our free persons .... that we are going to do our part in seeing that a majority of citizens understand the economic facts of life, the proper working of our system toward its good ends, and the fallacy of all these contrary something-for-nothing fairy tales .... that we ourselves are then going to act with economic and political horse—sense in our daily business and personal lives, and that we are publicly going to encourage an increasing majority of citizens to insist very vocally on their representatives acting with the same economic and political horse-sense toward the greatest and surest further attainment of our material and spiritual needs and desires.

And let us businessmen stop being Nervous Nellies about this! There is no such thing as a humiliating defeat in a just cause. And, anyhow, let's go at this job fearlessly—recognizing that mightier than armies is the power of a righteous idea whose time has come.

So let's boldly take—and continue from there on—the leadership that's expected of people like us in this patriot's job of standing up, speaking out, and being counted—no matter who has to be contradicted!

21 REPRISE

Let us attempt to summarize what we have been saying about the problem and its solution. Private business was being misjudged by the public in very important respects. Misunderstanding on the part of the majority was almost total. Even the minority—including too many investors and managers—lacked the necessary understanding in too high a degree.

The cause of this was twofold. First, there had been a dearth of education about the great good that private business had accomplished in providing more and better products at more attractive prices than would have been possible from government-owned and -operated production and distribution. Second, the public had gained an erroneous impression from the brute, crook, and exploiter charge hurled so relentlessly by the enemies of business through direct and conveniently available indirect channels.

Entirely too many citizens wrongly assumed they were unaffected bystanders, mere witnesses to a battle between the enemies and the owners of private business.

Because of the prevailing misunderstanding, the public itself, actively and passively, was preventing private business from being anywhere near as useful as it otherwise could have been to each member of the public in his role as worker, buyer, seller, saver, and otherwise affected citizen.

Who was at fault for this absurd and self-contradictory situation? The public itself! That is, each member of the public, regardless of station! Even the "nobody told me" excuse was no defense. When the citizen had the privilege of making his own decisions as to what to do in his own interests, and failed to become competent and remain alert in making those decisions correctly, he could only expect to lose the privilege and find himself being told what to do by a dictatorial government. Whether or not he had help was beside the point. It was his personal responsibility to dig out the pertinent facts—without help, if necessary—and to withstand persuasion from any source that the hard facts were different from what he had found them to be.

History was strewn with the wrecks of attempts at popular government which had failed because the majority of the citizens did not understand the duties that went with the privileges of freedom and thus failed to see through misrepresentation and make wisely the decisions delegated to them. The problem was the same in any private business, since its effectiveness in the common interest depended on the correctness and strength of the economic and moral motivation—together with the ability to resist demagoguery—of the voluntary participants in their pursuit of their own individual interests.

Yet, although it was up to the individual citizen to seek out the truth for himself, the sad fact was this: If the majority kept hearing and believing just one side, and did not get responsible and persuasive help in learning what the other side could justifiably claim, everyone would suffer a further sharp reduction in both his material and his nonmaterial well-being.

General Electric was inevitably being affected. Because of the antibusiness propaganda, it was not receiving the cooperation it so badly needed. This lessened its ability to offer good values and jobs and to make other contributions to the well-being of everyone concerned. The problem was how to help our contributor-claimants stop inflicting harm upon themselves and begin cooperating with each other toward those good ends which they really desired.

The General Electric manager—at every level—clearly and inescapably had an individual responsibility to do his part to end this pointless resistance to progress in values, jobs, and other benefits. That responsibility was a dual one. First, as an affected citizen, he like other citizens had the responsibility to do what he could to remove the causes for such resistance. Second, as a manager charged with helping the contributor-claimants to serve their own balanced-best-interests, it was his duty to make sure there were no valid reasons for resistance and also to help convince employees and others that they themselves would benefit by cooperating.

Where a manager saw contributor-claimants being misled into acting contrary to their own interests in the area of their company association or other mutual concern, and where he had access to corrective information and believed they did not, he became a party to the deceit and consequent injury to their interests if he did not supply the information, no matter who had to be contradicted.

How was the individual manager to do his part? The course seemed plainly to be this: First, he must objectively seek out anything that was in fact wrong and should be fixed, correct it promptly, and make it widely known that remedial action had been accomplished in keeping with the expressed values and wishes of those concerned. Second, he must determine what was erroneously believed to be wrong, supply the information necessary to convince the contributor-claimants that they had been misled, and then go beyond this to show them why it was in their own interest to extend their wholehearted cooperation to the common endeavor.

The pursuit of this course vastly increased the load on the manager both on and off the job. He had to study economics and marketing, and read related books, at home. He had to rearrange the order of priority in which he used his time on the job. And he had to find ways of delegating to subordinates some duties that he had formerly believed he must handle personally.

To achieve the objectivity necessary to the proper evaluation of upward communication about dissatisfactions or doubts, and to get on the same wave length in the two-way communication, he had to master, and be sure any manager responsible to him mastered, the still relatively new "you" approach as opposed to the "me" approach. This was necessary if he was to be sure of doing all that was humanly possible toward pleasing the contributor-claimants their way.

To be credible in the human relationships—and to have those concerned reject the brute charge in their own interest—the manager had to keep human considerations uppermost in his mind at all times. He had to prove he was doing so not only by his direct words, acts, and interest but also by his other activities on and off the job and even by what his face reflected when in repose.

To persuade all concerned that he was trying to do right voluntarily in the material area—and was not a member of a group of crooks and exploiters—he had to demonstrate his competence to make decisions or recommendations which were genuinely in the balanced-best-interests of all concerned. This required him to school himself in job economics and company economics to the point where he not only understood himself but was a persuasive teacher and advocate. The time, study, and practice required to reach and maintain competence in this area made this the toughest part of the expanded program for most managers.

Two difficulties faced the manager in meeting the new requirements for oral, written, and silent communication in the areas that had been more or less neglected. First, he had to become a good, or at least adequate, communicator in these areas. Second, he had to discipline himself to take the time required to do all of it well: in particular, he had to take all the time that was needed to be an unhurried listener and thinker when in two-way communication about something of importance to the other fellow. Available mass communication media were used by headquarters as much as possible to shorten the personal time required of the individual manager. But the residue of need for vocal communications by the individual manager was still so great that he found himself having to pass down some of the work he had formerly done in the areas less directly linked with the efforts to secure cooperation.

In seeking to demonstrate to contributor-claimants the reasons why they would find it rewarding to cooperate with one another, the manager might be aided or opposed by union officials. This would depend on whether the manager and his associates, by their teachings and conduct, had succeeded in making it "good politics"—with the majority of union members and the public—for the union officials to speak and act favorably about such cooperation.

Government officials at all levels—regardless of their personal feelings—would likewise be forced by the hard rules of politics to aid or oppose the manager's efforts. Again, this would depend on whether the manager had succeeded in making it "good politics" with the majority of their constituents for the officials to support the cooperation.

As the record shows, this effort at enlightened cooperation was undertaken by thousands of General Electric managers and their professional associates, and by countless other self-appointed but most welcome thought-leaders within and beyond the company's walls. Naturally there was a wide variation in individual courage, understanding, aptitude, and zeal. There were some outright unbelievers and a few very regrettable failures of the kind that are inevitable in human affairs. But the vast majority made the effort and obtained gratifying results. As a general rule, the gain in cooperation achieved by the individual manager was in proportion to the quality and faithfulness of his effort—which means, of course, that opportunities facing all managers were pretty much the same.

Clearly demonstrated by our efforts were two facts that were a source of utmost gratification and encouragement to me. First, the average citizen in or out of our business was ready to listen to anyone who would patiently and sensibly offer pertinent facts and sober opinions bearing on controversial questions. Second, the average citizen, by and large, could and would make sound economic and moral decisions for his own and the common good when he was given access, over a long enough period, to the full facts and claims on both sides of any job-connected or company-connected or community-connected question.

As must long since have become evident, all this proved a rewarding experience for me personally. I am enormously grateful for having had the privilege of passing that way.

TOPICAL INDEX

173

About the Author

Lemuel R. Boulware is a native of Springfield, Ky., and a graduate of the University of Wisconsin, where he taught accounting and commercial law briefly after graduation.

For his services as Operations Vice Chairman of the War Production Board in World War II he was awarded the Presidential Medal of Merit and a citation by the Navy.

In the course of a varied business career Mr. Boulware was successively marketing manager of the Easy Washing Machine Company, vice president and general manager of Carrier Corporation, vice president and general manager of Celotex Corporation, and vice president and general manager of General Electric Company's wholly owned manufacturing subsidiaries. As vice president in the relations area for the 14 years preceding his retirement from General Electric on January 1, 1961, Mr. Boulware helped GE pioneer new concepts and practices in its relations with employees, unions, stockholders, governments, and community neighbors.

He is the holder of four honorary degrees: Doctor of Science, Doctor of Humane Letters, and Doctor of Laws (2).